Benny,

I have being working with Jehan, & until I got this book, I had no idea how much his high achieving had effected him.

I read it in one night & cried as I thought of you.

I love you. Mama x

Jehan Casinader is a New Zealand journalist with a career spanning 12 years in primetime TV current affairs. He has reported for TVNZ's flagship programmes, including *Sunday*, *Seven Sharp*, *Close Up* and *Breakfast*.

In the aftermath of natural disasters, terror attacks, sporting triumphs and everything in between, Jehan has helped hundreds of people to share their vulnerable and deeply personal stories. He was named Broadcast Reporter of the Year at the Voyager Media Awards in 2020, and Reporter of the Year at the New Zealand Television Awards in 2018.

THIS IS ~~HOW IT ENDS~~
<u>NOT</u> HOW IT ENDS

THIS IS ~~HOW IT ENDS~~ NOT HOW IT ENDS

JEHAN CASINADER

HarperCollinsPublishers

HarperCollinsPublishers
Australia • Brazil • Canada • France • Germany • Holland • Hungary
India • Italy • Japan • Mexico • New Zealand • Poland • Spain • Sweden
Switzerland • United Kingdom • United States of America

First published in 2020
by HarperCollins*Publishers* (New Zealand) Limited
Unit D1, 63 Apollo Drive, Rosedale, Auckland 0632, New Zealand
harpercollins.co.nz

Copyright © Jehan Casinader 2020

Jehan Casinader asserts the moral right to be identified as the author of this work. This work is copyright. All rights reserved. No part of this publication may be reproduced, copied, scanned, stored in a retrieval system, recorded, or transmitted, in any form or by any means, without the prior written permission of the publisher.

A catalogue record for this book is available from the National Library of New Zealand.

ISBN 978 1 7755 4156 1 (hardback)
ISBN 978 1 7754 9187 3 (ebook)
ISBN 978 1 4607 8591 1 (audio book)

Cover and endpaper design by George Saad, HarperCollins Design Studio
Author photograph by Mike Heydon / Jet Productions
Typeset in Sabon LT Std by Kirby Jones
Printed and bound in Australia by McPherson's Printing Group

The papers used by HarperCollins in the manufacture of this book are a natural, recyclable product made from wood grown in sustainable plantation forests. The fibre source and manufacturing processes meet recognised international environmental standards, and carry certification.

To my best friend, Tommy Livingston,
for holding a torch while the road was dark.

CONTENTS

HELLO	1
WHERE TO GET HELP	9

I. RECLAIM YOUR STORY

1. TERROR	13
2. PAIN	26
3. STORIES	40
4. AUTHOR	52

II. REWRITE YOUR PAST

5. TRAUMA	67
6. SCARS	79
7. SCRIPTS	90

III. REINVENT YOUR CHARACTER

8. IDENTITY	105
9. CONNECTION	118
10. SUFFERING	132
11. MOTIVATION	147

IV. RESHAPE YOUR PLOT

12. CONFLICT	163
13. MEANING	176
14. CONTAGION	189
15. ENDINGS	201

V. RELEASE YOUR ENDING

16. TRUST	215
17. ACCEPTANCE	226
18. FREEDOM	236

EPILOGUE	248
THANKS	251
STORY GUIDE	253

"There is no greater agony than bearing an untold story inside you."

– Zora Neale Hurston

HELLO

I'm thinking about you right now, and I have so many questions. Who are you, I wonder? What's on your face? Is it curiosity, frustration, pain – or hope? I want to know: Where did you get this book? Maybe you discovered it in a library, or a garage, or the bargain bin at your local bookstore. Maybe some do-gooder gave it to you, hoping it'll fix you.

No matter how the book came into your hands, I'm pleased it did. Before you read on, there are a few things I should mention. I'm not a doctor. I'm not a counsellor. I'm not a psychologist, or a psychiatrist, or a psychotherapist (or a psychic). I can't prescribe anything stronger than a well-brewed cup of Ceylon tea.

But there are two things I *am* qualified in. Firstly, I'm an expert on living at the bottom of a very deep hole. I'm a survivor of depression. I don't mean "feeling blue" or being "down in the dumps". I'm talking about intense, unrelenting, suicidal depression – four whole years of it. Secondly, I know a few things about storytelling. As a journalist for TVNZ, I have made a living for 12 years by telling stories about real people. I've encountered the very best – innovators, scientists, athletes and artists – and the very worst – killers, abusers, fraudsters and neo-Nazis. (Oh, and The Jonas Brothers. I'll let you decide which category to put them in.) Being a journalist has allowed me to document the most extraordinary moments in these people's lives.

But the stories that really hook me – the ones that matter most – are about ordinary people who have been pushed to their limits. From the start of my career, I was drawn to stories about tragedy, pain and loss. As a fresh-faced young reporter, I was fascinated by people who had survived huge challenges. But I was a detached observer. At the end of each shoot, once the lights were packed away, I would get in the car with the camera operator and drive home thinking, *I'm so glad that will never be me.* However, at the age of 26, my own life began to spin out of control.

At first, depression came as a trickle. Then a torrent. Then a flood. It seeped into every corner of my life and destroyed many of the things that were important to me. I tried every mental health tool I could find, from meditation to medication. Most of those efforts made very little difference to my state of mind. After a couple of years, there seemed to be only one simple, appealing option left: taking my own life. I knew how much pain it would cause my friends and family, but I also believed an illness had colonised my brain. Just like a cancer patient, I was sick. I could fight back, but if my depression killed me, I couldn't possibly be held responsible.

Like many people who experience mental distress, I tried to hide the fact that I was struggling. I was ashamed that I couldn't sort myself out and worried that my depression would jeopardise my career. For a long time, I kept it a secret from almost everyone – including my colleagues at TVNZ. I put on a brave face and did my job to the best of my ability. Whether I was interviewing the prime minister or reporting from the scene of the Christchurch terror attack, I was determined to push through. Eventually, my suicidal thoughts became overwhelming, and every day I spent most of my energy trying to keep those thoughts under control. I knew that this couldn't last.

As I hurtled towards oblivion, I realised there was one thing I hadn't tried: storytelling. As a reporter, I had met hundreds of people who had overcome adversity. I interviewed Daniel Rockhouse, the hero of the Pike River Mine disaster, and Karina Andrews, the sexual abuse survivor who sent her dad to jail. And who could forget Liam Malone, the guy who lost both legs but turned himself into a blade-running Paralympian? Each of these people chose to *rewrite* their life stories. They created new narratives that explained who they were, where they had come from and where they were going. These narratives helped them to recover from mental distress.

I began to wonder: Could I do the same? Rather than trying to fix or cure my depression, what if I changed the story that I had wrapped around it? I embarked on an experiment to do just that. I reclaimed my life story. I rewrote my past. I reinvented my character. I reshaped my plot. And I released control of my ending. In the chapters ahead, I'll walk you through each of these five steps. I'll introduce you to the incredible people I met along the way. And I'll help you to explore your own life story. By the end of this book, I hope you will have the tools to be a better author of your story – and a better character in it. At the back, on page 253, there's a handy guide to help you with that process.

*

New Zealand is facing a mental health crisis, and we have spent more than a decade trying to address it. Kiwis have become much better at talking about our problems and asking for help. We have begun to reduce the shame and stigma around conditions like depression and anxiety. More money has been pumped into our public health system. And yet, in the year to 30 June 2019, there were 685 people who took their own lives in New Zealand – the highest number on record, and almost double the road toll. Our suicide rates for men and teenagers are among the worst in the world. It's clear that some of our strategies to tackle this crisis are just not working for enough people.

Clinical diagnoses such as "depression" can be really helpful. But they can also act as blunt labels that don't reveal the true causes of our distress, and don't provide many clues about how to get well. We all experience distress in unique ways, and there's no one-size-fits-all model for treatment. We need to be bold, and try new tools that can help us to overcome suffering and, if necessary, learn how to live with it. One of those tools is storytelling. This book is not a silver bullet, and it can't replace the advice of a mental health professional. But I hope I can give you a new framework for thinking about mental distress.

Parts of the book are pretty raw. You will meet people whose stories feature confronting themes, including suicidality, sexual violence and childhood abuse. While you're reading, please remember that all of these people made it through. They survived. They are telling their stories from a place of strength and health. However, this material may be triggering for you. It may bring back memories from your past, or highlight the challenges you are facing right now. If so, I strongly encourage you to share your thoughts and feelings with a trusted friend, family member or professional. I have included a list of free support services at the end of this note, on page 9.

I have no idea where you are in your journey. You may be experiencing depression or anxiety. You may have had suicidal thoughts and bravely fought them for months, years, even decades. If so, you're not alone. I hope you can take courage from the following pages. I'm also aware that some readers may not have been through any form of mental distress. Perhaps you're supporting a loved one who is going through a tough time. Make no mistake, this book is for you too. Everyone has a story that matters.

Before we begin, a word on empathy. It means to step into someone else's shoes. You're not walking in their shoes as *you*. You're walking in their shoes as *them*. I challenge you to disengage your brain and engage your heart. You may disagree with parts of this book, and some of my ideas may not reflect your own life experience. That's okay. But, as I share my story, I encourage you to scrutinise your own. Doing so can feel vulnerable and scary, but I guarantee that you'll be surprised by what you discover. If this book sheds a little light in a dark corner, please count that as a win. And, if it seems like I'm jumping around a bit, please forgive me. Life rarely unfolds in a perfect way, and nor does this book. (The events are not all written in the order in which they occurred.) I hope you'll stay with me until the last chapter.

You know, I never imagined I'd be depressed. I never imagined I'd be desperate to end my own life. And I certainly never imagined that the mental health stories I often covered on TV would eventually become *my* story.

But, if there is anything I have learnt so far, it is this: no matter how bad it gets, you have the power to craft your own life story – and no one can take that away from you. One of the main things that separates those who survive mental distress from those who don't is their ability to become great authors. Even in their darkest moments, those people have the confidence to say, "This is not how it ends."

WHERE TO GET HELP

If you are worried about your safety, please contact your local mental health crisis team, or go to the emergency department of your nearest hospital.

If you are in immediate danger, phone 111 in New Zealand or 000 in Australia.

Other confidential, free support services are listed below. These are run by trained counsellors and volunteers. They're available 24 hours a day. If you don't get the help you need the first time, please keep trying.

NEW ZEALAND

National mental health helpline: Call or text 1737

Youthline: Call 0800 376 633, text 234 or email talk@youthline.co.nz

Depression helpline: Call 0800 111 757, text 4202 or visit depression.org.nz for resources

Lifeline Aotearoa: Call 0800 LIFELINE (0800 543 354) or text HELP (4357)

Safe To Talk: The national sexual harm helpline; call 0800 044 334, text 4334 or visit safetotalk.nz

Suicide Crisis Helpline: Call 0508 TAUTOKO (0508 828 865)

AUSTRALIA
Beyond Blue: Support for depression and anxiety; call 1300 22 4636 or visit beyondblue.org.au

Lifeline: Call 13 11 14 or visit lifeline.org.au

Headspace: For young people; call 1800 650 890 or visit headspace.org.au

1800 RESPECT: For those affected by sexual abuse or violence; phone 1800 RESPECT (1800 737 732) or visit 1800respect.org.au

Suicide Callback Service: Call 1300 659 467 or visit suicidecallbackservice.org.au

I. Reclaim your story

1. TERROR

I wanted to go home. It was a slow Friday afternoon in TVNZ's Auckland newsroom. Around 3 pm, I stuck my head into an edit suite to tell my boss, Jane, that I was heading off for the weekend. She glanced up from her computer and said, "Have you heard about the shooting?" I stared at her blankly. Somewhere in the foggy recesses of my brain, a little man was riding a bicycle very fast, searching for the information I needed. *Shooting? What shooting? Was I meant to be shooting a story this weekend?* Jane interrupted those thoughts. "In Christchurch," she said. "At the mosque."

I pulled out my phone. The bright red BREAKING NEWS banners were just beginning to curl around the home pages of the news websites. A gunman had opened fire during Friday prayers at Al Noor Mosque. There were unconfirmed reports that dozens were injured. *A terror attack? In Christchurch?* This seemed too outlandish to be true. At worst, I thought, it was a cruel hoax. At best, it was a wild rumour. But, as the news sites began spewing out more detailed updates, we knew that this story was legit – and it was unfolding in real time. A second shooting had just taken place at Linwood Mosque on the other side of the CBD, and the gunman was possibly heading to a third location. "I think we should go," I said.

I raced downstairs to the newsroom. There was total chaos. A special live programme had just begun, with ashen-faced reporters standing outside a police cordon near Al Noor Mosque. I glanced at the wall of screens above the newsroom, and could see raw footage coming into our server, showing injured people being carried on stretchers out of ambulances and into Christchurch Hospital. I couldn't watch for very long, because the *Sunday* team was swinging into action. Our cameraman, Martin, raced off to pack his gear. He would meet me at the airport. Producers booked flights and accommodation, and scoured social media for any scraps of information that could tell us who the gunman was and what his motivation might be. I ordered an Uber to take me to the airport, where I would jump on the next plane.

As I walked out of the TVNZ building, my phone pinged. A friend sent me a Facebook message: *It was live-streamed. I've been sent the link. I can send it to you if you want? Be careful. Sounds like he is still shooting people.* I glanced at the time. If I was quick, I could squeeze in a few more minutes in the office. I cancelled my Uber, sprinted back to my desk, and gathered a few colleagues. I turned my phone sideways and pressed play. We watched the gunman carry his firearms up the front steps of Al Noor Mosque. A man greeted him with the words, "Hello, brother." Moments later, there were screams – not just in the video, but also around my desk. One senior reporter, who has covered the toughest stories in the country, grabbed my arm instinctively. Her fingernails dug into my skin as we watched the gunman take his first shots.

There was no question: We would have to scrap that weekend's *Sunday* programme, which had already been taped, and produce a story about the attack. Usually, I had three or four weeks to research, film, script and edit a segment. This time, I had 48 hours. On the way to the airport, I stopped by my flat and threw a bunch of clothes into a suitcase. By the time I was on the motorway, just after 4 pm, Prime Minister Jacinda Ardern had begun a press conference. "This is one of New Zealand's darkest days," she said. "Clearly, what has happened here is an extraordinary and unprecedented act of violence. Many of those who would have been directly affected by this shooting may be migrants to New Zealand. They may even be refugees here. They have chosen to make New Zealand their home, and it is their home. They are us."

My phone pinged again, with a text from a colleague: *IMPORTANT: The gunman is on the loose – possibly in a silver Subaru Outback. We have video of him shooting as he drives. BE VERY CAREFUL AND AWARE.*

As I boarded the plane to Christchurch, my heart was racing. In the air, there was silence – and no Wi-Fi for an hour. Just before takeoff, I had been sent a copy of "The Great Replacement", a manifesto that the gunman had published online. As I ate my Cookie Time in-flight snack, I read his rambling diatribe: a zealot's ode to white supremacy.

I had been a journalist for a decade, and often found myself in dangerous situations. I'd been abused, harassed and stalked. I'd visited drug dens and gang pads. I'd covered fires, floods and earthquakes. Danger was part of the gig. But, for the first time in my career, I was genuinely afraid for my physical safety. This assignment was deeply personal. The gunman was in the process of killing people who looked just like me.

*

Many people can tell a dreamy story about how their parents met. Maybe they were high-school sweethearts or university buddies. Want to hear about my parents? They met in a refugee shelter. In the early 1980s, Sri Lanka was in the grip of a bloody civil war. The government, dominated by the Sinhalese ethnic group, was fighting an insurgency of minority Tamils, known as the Tamil Tigers. Most ordinary citizens – including my Tamil parents – had nothing to do with the conflict. My mum, Saro, was a banker and my dad, Ravi, was a newspaper journalist. They came from well-educated families. But, in a war that divides two cultures, none of that matters. No matter where you live, what you earn or what you do, if you're in the wrong place at the wrong time, you may end up on the wrong side of a gun.

Journalists were in more danger than other citizens. My dad was once taken in for questioning at a government building in which people were sometimes tortured. He was never harmed, but others were not so lucky. In what became known as "white van disappearances", journalists were abducted and taken away in vehicles with no number plates. They never came home to their families. Other media figures were assassinated in broad daylight. The violence drove many Sri Lankans out of their homeland in search of safety. My parents came to

New Zealand as immigrants in the late 1980s, following other members of our extended family who had already settled here. I was born in Aotearoa, and so was my younger brother, Prashan. This is the only home we have ever known.

Our grandma lived with us, and took care of my brother and me while our parents worked hard – as most immigrants do – to give us the very best opportunities. My mum worked in government policy, and my dad worked at *The Dominion* at night and studied law during the day. He became a solicitor. Neither of my parents could tell me how rugby was played, but around our dinner table, we talked about politics, identity and social justice. I learnt how hard it was for them to adapt to life in this country. They spoke about the discrimination they faced in their workplaces. They recalled the many times people asked, "Where did you learn to speak such good English?" not realising that Sri Lanka was colonised by the British. My parents really missed their homeland; the place where they truly belonged. Because of their sacrifices, I wanted to make something of my life. I became a journalist so that I would have the power to tell stories that mattered. In New Zealand, I thought I could do my job safely, and that I would never be targeted because of the colour of my skin.

TERROR

*

On 15 March 2019, I landed in Christchurch at dusk. The airport was swarming with armed police. Our crew grabbed a rental car and headed for the hospital, where a Muslim community leader took me to the floor where the families of the injured had gathered. There was crying, weeping, total confusion. It was a similar scene at the police cordon on Deans Avenue, near Al Noor Mosque. As night fell, local Muslims were desperate to access the mosque. In their faith, burials should take place within 24 hours of death. But the mosque was a crime scene, and the bodies lying inside had not been formally identified. It was still unclear who had died, and who had escaped. I met Zuhair Darwish, who was looking for his brother, Kamel, a 38-year-old Jordanian farm worker who had moved to New Zealand six months earlier. I watched as Zuhair kept ringing Kamel's phone, but he couldn't reach him.

In the early hours of Saturday morning, we checked in to a hotel to get a couple of hours' sleep. Before dawn, we returned to those dark streets – and decided to take a punt. Rather than heading to the spot where all the other TV cameras were positioned, we would drive around the back of Hagley Park and approach the mosque on foot.

It would be a 20-minute walk while carrying our gear. But, in television, if you don't have good pictures, you don't have a story. The gamble paid off and, remarkably, we could walk right into Hagley Park. "I was wondering how long it would take for you guys to work that out," came a voice from the shadows. It was an armed officer, keeping watch from beneath a tree. Moments later, I was standing directly opposite the mosque. Outside, there were bodies covered by tarpaulins. Blood was pouring down the entranceway. Martin turned his camera on. "So, this is it," I said, looking down the lens. "The entrance to Al Noor Mosque. The very steps that the gunman walked down yesterday afternoon."

A police boss strode up to us. "Is that on?" he asked, pointing at the camera. Martin swung the lens away. "Look. There are bodies in there," the officer said. "I want you to think very carefully about what you're doing." I explained to him that we were in a public place, that we had a legal right to film, and that we would carefully select which clips to broadcast. He walked away disgruntled, but I didn't care. The media are meant to be truth-tellers, and the truth was that 51 people were dead. They were killed in a racially motivated hate crime. Every night, we broadcast images from disasters and war zones around the world. Just because this massacre happened at home, why would we sanitise it?

Kiwis needed to know what had taken place in their own backyard.

Late on Saturday night, I checked in to another hotel room and began writing my script. Staring at a blank screen and a flashing cursor, I felt like my journalistic instincts had vanished. I was so tired that I couldn't switch into the "reporter voice" that was so familiar to me. All I could do was talk to the audience as a human. I began my voiceover: "How can one day make us feel so much – make us angry, make us proud, make us hurt? How can one day change the face of our country forever?" I allowed myself to sleep from 1 am to 3 am, then I continued writing on my laptop as we headed to Christchurch Airport for the red-eye flight back to Auckland.

I finished the script at 8 am on Sunday, just as our taxi pulled up to TVNZ. There, much of our team had gathered, armed with coffee. We had a few hours to edit a story that would usually take a week to splice together. My brilliant producer, Paul, who had been with me in Christchurch, started putting the item together with the editor, Debbie. As the day progressed, we faced a slew of important questions from our colleagues. "What shall we put in the presenter's intro?" "Do we need to blur that person's face?" "Is that person's name spelt right?" "Do we need to run a warning about the violence?"

"That guy you interviewed at the police cordon – do you know whether they found his brother?" The last question stood out to me. I sent a text to Zuhair: *Any news about your brother today, Zuhair?* A devastatingly sparse reply came back instantly: *He's one of the dead ones.*

Our deadline was approaching fast, but for a moment, I didn't care. I stared out of the window behind my desk, gazing at an empty intersection. A man had lost his brother. Dead. Gone. Forever. I was hit by a wave of emotions. Anger, disgust … and guilt. Dozens of people had been murdered, and I was only telling a story about it. Was that really the best I could do? The answer, frustratingly, was yes. Just a story. Nothing more, nothing less. I needed to do my job. We finished our report, entitled "Black Friday", at 6.52 pm, just over half an hour before the programme aired. That night, more than 500,000 people watched our snapshot of the 24 hours that had followed the massacre. We had given a voice to those who were deeply affected. We had crossed the finish line.

*

People often ask me, "Why is the news so negative?" I usually reply with another question: "Why do you slow down and rubberneck at crash sites?" We all do it. It's not out of genuine concern for the drivers and passengers, who have invariably been taken to hospital already. Instead, we want to cast our eyes upon the mangled wreck. To imagine what happened, and why. To imagine the person behind the wheel, which way they must have turned, and where they must have ended up. Humans can be so voyeuristic. We have a morbid fascination with tragic events in the lives of strangers, often because those events reinforce our own fears and anxieties. Our brains, which try to protect us, are sensitive to potential threats. That's why bad news sells. But I reckon there's another reason why we're drawn to stories about death and destruction: they remind us that we're still alive.

In every civilisation, people have found different ways to highlight the fragility of life. During victory parades in Ancient Rome, it was customary for a commander to ride through the streets sitting on a chariot. Over his shoulder, a slave would whisper in his ear in Latin, "*Memento mori ... Memento mori ...*" ("Remember that you will die"). As the commander looked out at the adoring citizens, he was being reminded that his power was only temporary. Despite wearing a crown, he was just as human as everyone else, and even the strongest army could not save him from the clutches of death. In more recent times, the term "memento mori" has been used to describe objects that remind us of our mortality, including skulls, hourglasses, clocks and dried flowers.

It may sound weird, but I reckon TV news is the memento mori of the modern age. Most news stories are grim – even depressing – but they also offer a powerful affirmation of life. When we catch a glimpse of someone else's distress, most of us turn inwards. We feel grateful for our relationships and the good things in our lives. We feel challenged to use our time and money in a positive way. Plenty of people have told me that after watching an emotional story on TV at night, they have walked into their children's bedrooms and hugged them as they slept. The news touches people on a very deep level. But it also leaves indelible marks on the journalists who capture it.

On the evening that I finished my story on the Christchurch terror attack, I left the TVNZ newsroom and walked home to my flat. My bedroom looked like a construction site. Clothes were strewn everywhere, untouched since the afternoon of the massacre. That felt like weeks ago, but was just 48 hours earlier. I threw myself onto my bed. For the first time in days, I was alone – and there was total silence. Now that my job was done, I could begin to process what had happened.

TERROR

I was hungry, lonely, tired and confused. As I stared at the ceiling, I was struck by a dark realisation. I had just reported on the deaths of 51 people, but the viewers had no idea that my own life was on the line.

Life is fragile.

2. PAIN

DO I CARE? When I started working in television, those three words were emblazoned on a massive sign that hung above my producer's desk. Each letter took up a whole A4 piece of paper. What he really meant was, "Does the audience care?" TV bosses are obsessed with the people who watch their shows. They have to be, because if the viewers don't care about a story – if it doesn't make them *feel* something – they won't watch it. They'll change the channel. If that happens too often, ratings fall, advertising drops, programmes are dumped, journalists get fired – and, worst of all, good stories aren't told. If it sounds like a brutal, cut-throat business, that's because it is. But I couldn't imagine a more thrilling industry to work in.

I was 20 years old when I scored my first proper job, reporting for a daily current affairs show called *Close Up*. Every night, Kiwis would tune in to find out what had happened in the country that day. The programme covered all the big events, and scored interviews with newsmakers. I wanted to make my mark. I was willing to crawl over broken glass to get my hands on a great story. I chased drug dealers, politicians and fraudsters down the street. I investigated important social issues like domestic violence, homelessness and the rise of synthetic drugs. I saw myself as a brown, modern-day Tintin – a professional observer of the world, and of people.

The weird thing about being on TV is that the audience can see you, but you can't see them. When you're staring at a camera, it's easy to forget that hundreds of thousands of people are on the other side of it. Despite choosing such a public job, I'm actually pretty shy. But being on TV is like putting on a superhero costume. It gives you courage. At 23, I joined a new, more relaxed show called *Seven Sharp*, which pushed me out of my comfort zone – and out of a plane in the very first episode. I ate insects on air. I sheared a sheep (badly). I rapped. I flipped burgers. I tried to be a cheerleader. I interviewed Prime Minister John Key dressed as a panda. (Just to be clear: I was the panda, not him – although he would have enjoyed wearing the costume more than I did.) I learnt not to take myself so seriously.

The job was exhausting, but no matter where I travelled, I knew that I would come home to a safe place.

Near Wellington's rugged south coast, I flatted with three of my closest mates. We did everything together: cooking, drinking, laughing, fighting, and having honest conversations about life. We had parties and played pranks. One morning, I woke up with a goldfish tank in my bedroom. Some nights, when we were feeling uncharacteristically rebellious, we would race our ageing sedans through the city. I don't just treasure these moments because I'm feeling nostalgic. At the time, I knew they were special. In our flat's kitchen, I hung up a print that declared: THESE ARE THE GOLDEN DAYS. After work, I would often drive to Island Bay and sit in my car, watching the sunset while listening to Massive Attack. I was grateful to have so many good things in my life. I was yet to learn that seasons never last.

*

At 26, I landed my dream job, reporting for TVNZ's top current affairs programme, *Sunday*. I grew up watching the show's formidable correspondents. Now, as the youngest reporter in *Sunday*'s 15-year history, I had a chance to learn from those brilliant storytellers and do meaningful work. The job was in Auckland, but I couldn't pass it up. I reluctantly said goodbye to my friends and family in Wellington – the only city I had ever known – and headed north in my trusty 1996 Mazda, which was packed with clothes and furniture. In Auckland, I hoped to build a new life pretty quickly. However, I soon realised that I was in way over my head. The job was stressful, and the stories were emotionally draining. I was finding my feet – alone – in a new city.

One night, I forced myself to go for a run. It took every ounce of strength to drag myself out of the house in search of an endorphin rush. Afterwards, I trudged home feeling glum and opened the door of my flat. I heard a rustling noise and flicked the light on. There, sitting at the dining table as if he was waiting for dinner, was the largest rat I had ever seen. I lunged as he leapt off the table, somersaulted in the air, flipped his middle claw at me (at least, that's how I remember it) and disappeared out of sight.

This was far from the glamorous TV life that people seemed to think I had. Most nights, I ate takeaways and drank cheap wine before going to bed, only to lie awake, consumed by a belief that I had screwed up my life. Even though I was exactly where I wanted to be, my success felt hollow. Many of my mates were entering a whole new life stage – getting married, buying houses and having kids. I was painfully aware that I had achieved none of those things, and felt like I was being left behind. I couldn't imagine what my future would look like, couldn't imagine finding someone who loved me or starting a family. I wondered if I had sacrificed those things for my career. Maybe I was destined to just keep making TV until I carked it.

In the early hours of a winter morning, I crawled out of bed and ventured into the rain. I had no shoes and no phone, but my car journey would be short. On nights when I couldn't sleep, I was drawn into the warm embrace of my local McDonald's. In the space of one year, I travelled beneath the golden arches a whopping 58 times, according to my bank statement. That's 58 Quarter Pounders, 58 cartons of medium fries and 348 nuggets. But on this morning, disaster struck: the 24/7 outlet was closed for renovations. I drove to another suburb and another dark, empty McDonald's. Frustrated, I tried a third restaurant, but it was also shut. Unable to face the prospect of walking into a service station to buy junk food – barefoot, partially clothed and likely to be arrested – I decided to go back to bed. Somewhere, I could hear Ronald McDonald laughing.

*

I had never seen a dead cat until the day I stepped inside Tokanui Psychiatric Hospital, near Hamilton. There it was – brown, dried-out, with its facial features still intact – lying in the middle of a corridor, next to an upturned gurney. The cat had probably been decomposing for years. Tokanui closed in 1998 and had been boarded up ever since. As I wandered the asbestos-ridden corridors, our cameraman, Byron, filmed the creepy remnants of Tokanui's past. There were isolation wards. Children's dolls and prams were scattered everywhere. The complex felt like the set of a horror movie, but for many Kiwis, this place was very real.

The hospital, which opened just before World War I, was built in the countryside on a 5000-acre piece of farmland. Tokanui became a small town in itself. It housed and treated up to 1000 mental health patients at a time, many of whom were classed as "insane" or "mentally unsound", or described as "lunatics". Many were experiencing conditions we now know as depression, anxiety and post-traumatic stress disorder. Around 500 patients died at Tokanui and were buried in unmarked graves in a paddock. My visit to the property reminded me that New Zealand's mental health system has a dark past. Until the 1980s and 1990s, powerful state-run institutions controlled the lives of our most vulnerable people. Former patients have claimed they experienced beatings, sexual abuse and non-consensual shock therapy at Tokanui and other psychiatric units.

Thankfully, the days of forced institutional care are almost gone – in New Zealand, at least. The idea of isolating or detaining someone simply because they are mentally unwell is now deemed a gross violation of their dignity and human rights. Advances in psychology have helped us to understand that most people experiencing mental distress have the best chance of recovery if they are treated with compassion within their own communities, and given independence. As a result, our homes, schools and workplaces are full of people who are facing mental health challenges while also living ordinary lives, without necessarily showing visible signs of distress to other people. That's a good thing, but it also means that some of us feel pressure to keep functioning at a "normal" level, even when we are struggling.

After six months of living in Auckland, I knew that I was in a bad space. I was fatigued, moody and miserable. I wasn't sure what was wrong with me, and I wondered if I was slipping into depression. But I was also determined to make sure that no one found out. I kept my distress a secret from my family and most of my friends, because I didn't want them to worry about me. I also hid it from my colleagues and bosses. At work, I was the new kid on the block, and everyone was watching to see how well I would perform. I had been hired to do a difficult job, and I didn't want anyone to think I couldn't hack it. Some days, however, it was hard to keep a brave face.

Inside TVNZ, down the longest corridor in the oldest, most dilapidated part of the building, there's a tiny nook called the Wellness Room. In its heyday, it was a green room for big stars who were about to go on TV. By the time I got there, it had become a sick bay and was the only room in the building that could be locked from the inside. There was nothing in there apart from an old couch, a lamp that didn't work and a box of tissues. On the afternoons when I was barely holding it together, I would lock myself in the Wellness Room and hide. There are only two things that go on in that room: napping and crying. Sometimes, I tried to do both at the same time.

*

Some years ago, a camera was sent on a mission inside my penis. (Don't read that sentence twice.) It was an awkward exercise and I wouldn't recommend it – for business or for pleasure. I had been in some pain, and my doctor wanted to check that there was nothing wrong in that department. Doctors, like journalists, are good at sending cameras into places they shouldn't really go. The human body can easily be poked, prodded and invaded in the name of medicine. Using scans, samples and tests, doctors can investigate the origins of physical pain. Technology allows them to draw conclusions with a fair amount of certainty. You'll be glad to know my manhood was found to be in good health.

But, although physical illness can often be examined in a robust way, mental illness is much trickier. Doctors can't "test" you for depression. Nor can they send a camera inside your brain. They can only make a diagnosis based on any symptoms you describe. Mental health professionals are guided by the *Diagnostic and Statistical Manual of Mental Disorders*, commonly known as the *DSM*. This handbook, published by the American Psychological Association and used by mental health professionals worldwide, lists a range of symptoms for depression. These include low mood, loss of pleasure, disturbed sleep, fatigue, change in appetite, feelings of worthlessness, loss of focus, a change in movements, and suicidal thoughts. If five symptoms stick around for at least a fortnight, you meet the criteria for "major depressive disorder".

According to the World Health Organization, depression is the world's leading cause of disability, affecting around 264 million people. Scientists have not identified an individual biological cause of depression. Research shows that genetics, brain chemistry and ageing may all influence whether someone develops depressive symptoms. But our current diagnostic model has extraordinary limitations. It focuses on a patient's symptoms, but does not take into account their life history or environment – their trauma, relationships and experiences. Nor does it account for the patient's characteristics – their personality, beliefs and values. Because of this, a depression diagnosis must be understood for what it is: a snapshot of what someone is experiencing at a particular point in time.

When I visited my doctor and heard him say, "It sounds like depression," I breathed a sigh of relief. I thought, *I'm not crazy. I have a real illness, with a name and a Wikipedia page. Other people have it too. Now I can get on with dealing with it*. But, on reflection, the word "depression" told me absolutely nothing about myself. It told me nothing about the source of my pain, or how to make it go away. All it told me was that something had gone wrong inside my head.

In the weeks that followed, this amorphous label began to define my whole existence. I thought I wasn't interested in seeing people because I had depression. I didn't want to exercise because I had depression. I wasn't enjoying work because I had depression. Even so, I knew that I was in charge of getting myself out of this rut.

Over a period of many months, I made gradual changes to my lifestyle. I improved my diet. I did more exercise. I drank less alcohol. I cut back on my social media use. I got more sleep. I learnt how to do Pilates from videos on YouTube. I took a yoga course. I went for massages. I started doing meditation and mindfulness activities. I took myself out for coffee. I volunteered at a food project for homeless people. I tried to make new friends. I read every self-help book, listened to every podcast and watched every TED Talk about depression. And I continued to push myself at work, hoping that, if all else failed, my job would save me. I felt more comfortable disappearing into other people's stories than confronting my own.

*

The sun was beating down in Christchurch when I sat with Maria Dillon on her back doorstep, preparing to film a story that was deeply personal for her. Maria's 18-year-old son, Harry McLean, had killed himself inside a mental health ward at Hillmorton Hospital. When I investigated Harry's death, I found clear failures in the care he had received from the hospital. This was an important story because Harry represented the many thousands of young people in the care of the mental health system. He had taken responsibility for his own wellbeing by asking for help, and had volunteered to stay in hospital because he didn't feel safe when he was by himself. Harry was let down by the system that was meant to protect him. Maria read me a note that her son had written in the lead-up to his death.

> "Can't concentrate ... Never have any energy ... I'm becoming more of a burden ... I derive no pleasure from friends ... I'm drinking too much ... I'm a hopeless wreck ... I don't like being so skinny ... I get agitated and annoyed ... There's nothing in life to look forward to."

One of the most tedious parts of making TV is having to ask people to do the same thing over and over. We had only one camera, and we needed to film Maria from several different angles, opening Harry's note and reading it aloud. It seemed unfair to ask her to do this, but she was gracious enough to understand that we needed the footage. As Maria read Harry's words again, they settled in my mind. *Burden ... No pleasure ... Hopeless ... Nothing to look forward to.* It felt like she was reading my own thoughts back to me. Harry's words – all of them – were exactly my own. The hopelessness, the sense of futility, the desire to find a way out – those ideas were in my head too. I had recently begun to have suicidal thoughts.

When I was growing up, suicide was a mystery to me – until I turned 16. That summer, one of my classmates killed himself during the school holidays. I don't remember what anyone said at his funeral, but I remember hearing songs by the Black Eyed Peas and Justin Timberlake pumping through the church speakers. As I stared at his casket, it all seemed so wrong. I wanted to make sense of his death. But, as anyone who has faced the aftermath of a suicide knows, it's impossible to make sense of an act that extinguishes life itself. When the new school year began, life moved on pretty quickly. Back then, suicide was never discussed – or even mentioned – in most schools. It was strictly taboo.

When I became a journalist, I took a special interest in reporting on suicide because I wanted to bring the issue into the national spotlight. In 2011, at the age of 21, I investigated a spate of teen suicides in Kawerau, a beautiful but impoverished milling town in the Bay of Plenty. I met parents who had lost children to suicide. A single mum stood with me in her son's bedroom – the place where he took his own life. She told me that he had just broken up with his first girlfriend, and couldn't see a hopeful future. That story deeply moved me. In the years that followed, I kept reporting on suicide, and discovered that it affects people from every walk of life. I interviewed farmers, businesspeople and celebrities who had buried their loved ones. I became familiar with the anguish, guilt and confusion that is felt by those who are left behind.

When I began having my own suicidal thoughts at the age of 27, I was well aware of the pain I would cause to other people if I took my own life. I wasn't *seriously* thinking about killing myself. I hadn't made a plan to do it, and I wasn't planning to make a plan. But those dark thoughts kept returning, gently beckoning me. And that was pretty scary. Despite all the effort I was putting into my mental health, I felt like I was entering a danger zone. But I wasn't willing to blindly accept that a chemical had gone haywire inside my brain. Even if that was the case, I was sure that my distress had originated somewhere else – not in my body, but in my life. I wanted to know where my pain was coming from.

Get curious about your pain.

3. STORIES

In January 2017, an orange man walked into the White House, and the world went nuts. How was it possible, many of us asked, that this ridiculous human had scored one of the most powerful jobs on the planet? Media pundits were dumbfounded. Over the previous year, they had painted a devastating picture of Donald Trump's ineptitude. They reported the lies he told during interviews. They highlighted the failures of his business empire. They investigated his secret tax records. They even dug up audio of him boasting about sexually assaulting women. The story of this man's life was so unflattering that it seemed obvious to many observers that he would lose the election. To them, Trump clearly lacked the dignity and character required of a president.

While the media was telling the story of the New York billionaire's impending downfall, he was on the campaign trail, telling his own story. And, true to form, that tale was larger than life. Once upon a time, Trump explained, there was a peaceful, prosperous nation called the United States of America. But that nation was ruined by a bunch of villains, including crooked politicians, slimy journalists and migrants who were rapists and terrorists. Trump assured his would-be voters that a hero was coming to save them – a hero wearing a bright red cap bearing the words MAKE AMERICA GREAT AGAIN. This story might not have resonated with the political elite in Washington, D.C., but it struck a chord in the baseball stadiums and county fairs of heartland America.

Trump tapped into the fear, pain and resentment that many Americans carried. He boldly claimed that he could restore the country to its supposed former glory. To many voters, that story was compelling – and hopeful. Cold, hard facts fell by the wayside. It didn't matter that the man had so many character flaws. Nor did it matter that he could barely explain how he would carry out his policies. In the end, it wasn't Trump's competence or political experience that won him the election. It was his ability to tell a persuasive story.

*

Stories are the building blocks of our lives. They inform us, entertain us, surprise us, delight us and help us to escape the drudgery of daily life. That's why we read fiction, go to the movies, play video games and watch trashy reality-TV. The internet allows us to consume more stories than ever before. By day, alerts on our smartphones pop and ping, vying for our attention. At night, we lie in bed, endlessly scrolling through our social media feeds. There is more content online than any of us could digest in a lifetime, but we can't turn away from it. We keep wanting more.

For millennia, humans have used stories to make sense of the world. Cavemen didn't draw pie charts or Venn diagrams on their walls; they told stories. Early Māori used waiata (songs), whakapapa (genealogy), whakataukī (proverbs) and haka (war chants) to tell stories. Children are introduced to the world by listening to stories. Family bonds are built around the dinner table, where everyone shares stories. The best advertising tells a story. At work, most of us would rather swap a PowerPoint presentation for a story. Stories help us to process and remember complex information. They form the connective tissue that holds our society together. In a wedding speech, you tell the story of a relationship. In a job interview, you tell the story of your career. At a funeral, you tell the story of a person's life. Storytelling is our default mode of understanding each other – and ourselves.

And yet, when I ring someone to ask for an interview, the most common response I get is, "Who, me? No, I don't have a story to tell." In New Zealand, that's no surprise. Kiwis are famously humble, and we're reluctant to stick our heads above the parapet. Tall poppy syndrome prevents us from speaking about our achievements and aspirations. We are terrified by the idea of blowing our own trumpet – especially in front of friends and family. But, as a journalist, I've learnt that people's reluctance to publicly share their stories goes much deeper than a fear of having their mug show up on national TV. Most people do not believe that their life stories have any *value* – no matter how interesting, unusual or important they may be.

Perhaps that's because our culture glorifies some people as gifted storytellers, like politicians, actors and celebrities – the people you often see holding microphones or loudspeakers. These people certainly have the gift of the gab, and they have access to powerful platforms from which they can speak to the masses. But do they have a monopoly on storytelling? No way. Each of us has a narrative that forms the basis of our life – a story that explains who we are, where we've come from and where we might be going. No one can opt out of storytelling, because we're hardwired for it. Rather than asking, "Do I have a story?" it's worth asking, "What kind of story am I telling?"

*

Dan P. McAdams, a psychology professor at Northwestern University in Illinois, is one of the world's top researchers in the field of narrative psychology. According to Dan, our personalities develop in layers. In early childhood, we learn to become "actors" in the world, with dispositional traits like curiosity, shyness, patience and determination. Then, as we grow into adolescence, we become "agents", developing our own goals and desires, and recognising that we have the power to make decisions that can effect change. Finally, we become "authors". We begin to see our lives as stories. Each of us is the main character in our own story – and also the author. In other words, your story is *about* you, but you're also in charge of *writing* it. Here's how Dan described it to me:

> "To be an agent is to feel that you have some control over what happens in your life. I can make decisions and carry them out. I'm not completely buffeted about by forces over which I have little control. Being an author goes beyond

that. It's about taking a step back and building a story around your life. That gives you another level of power. Not only can you make things happen in the world, but you can interpret them in a way that benefits you."

A baby doesn't realise that it is a character in a story. But, between the ages of three and five, kids become developmentally advanced enough to gather their thoughts and memories, and assemble them in a narrative form. Young children tell stories that are simple and chronological. ("And then I went to the park ... And then I had an ice cream ... And then I saw a unicorn ...") As they get older, children develop the cognitive abilities – and the necessary language – to tell more complex, nuanced stories. They learn to join the dots between events and ideas. By adolescence, they can identify patterns or themes in their stories. By adulthood, they understand deeper narrative concepts, like the idea that life is a "journey", that they have a "task", or that there is a desired end to the story. Without storytelling, life is just a random series of independent events. It is only by arranging those events into stories that we can interpret them in a meaningful way.

When I tell the story of my life, I imagine that I am telling the "right" version of it – the *only* version. I feel like I am playing back a tape recording, with every detail captured exactly as it happened. According to Dan, that's not how it works. He points out that our stories are not fixed; in fact, they're constantly evolving. Memories can change dramatically, depending on how they are recalled, interpreted and articulated. Some details are left out. Other parts are added, emphasised, diminished, edited or distorted. As the years go by, parts of a story will be forgotten, and other parts will be embellished.

This simple fact is staggering, because it reveals that our life stories are not necessarily "true". Nor are they "false". They're just stories, reflecting how we have chosen to interpret the events in our lives. It's a little unsettling to know that our stories are so fluid. But it also means that we have the power to construct them in a way that is useful to us. Although we can't change what has happened in our lives, we can use storytelling to find meaning in those events. Dan calls this process "autobiographical reasoning".

> "Life does not come to us naturally as a story. It doesn't have a pre-baked narrative form to it. But we have to make meaning out of what happens to us. People have been telling stories since the advent of language, so it makes good

sense to promote storytelling that contributes to psychological wellbeing."

Over the past 30 years, Dan and his team have interviewed hundreds of adults and analysed their life stories. From those stories, some common themes have emerged. One is "redemption" – the idea that positive meanings can be found in negative events, or that good things can come from bad experiences. Dan's research shows that people who tell redemptive stories about their lives have greater psychological wellbeing. They report higher levels of life satisfaction and have better self-esteem. These people are also more likely to be "generative", meaning they want to make a valuable contribution to the world and its future.

Other people tell stories that feature a lot of "contamination" – the idea that good things can be ruined by bad events. Dan says contamination is the opposite of redemption. It reflects despair and hopelessness. He discovered a link between this kind of storytelling and poor psychological wellbeing. People who tell their stories in a way that features a lot of contamination are more likely to report depressive symptoms. They also have lower life satisfaction and poorer self-esteem. These findings are important because they point to a strong connection between our stories and our mental health.

*

When I became depressed, I felt like I was walking through a library that contained a catalogue of my misery. There were rows and rows of books that described all the bad stuff that had happened in my life. Every moment when I was hurt. Every mistake I made. Every opportunity I missed. It was all right there, in black and white. As my mental health deteriorated, I found myself spending more time among those shelves, ruminating on how much pain I had experienced – and how much I had caused. Eventually, I was practically living in that library. I couldn't put those books down, and I believed that everything I was reading was true.

Here's the million-dollar question: Was I telling a bleak story about my life because I was depressed, or was I depressed because I was telling a bleak story? Jonathan M. Adler, a clinical psychologist and psychology professor at Olin College of Engineering in Massachusetts, has been exploring that chicken-and-egg question. In a 2012 study, Jonathan followed 47 people during a course of psychotherapy. After each session, participants wrote detailed narratives about their lives. Jonathan found that their stories began to change *before* their mental health improved. He concluded that therapy helped the participants to rewrite their narratives in a way that gave them a sense of power. Then, in Jonathan's words, they "lived *into* those new stories". For example, an 18-year-old girl described herself as "messed up" and "disappointed in myself" at the start of therapy, but over the 12-week course, her story gradually became more positive – and *then* her mental health scores improved. By the end of the course, she wrote that she was "EMPOWERED for GREATNESS!"

In a separate study, published in 2015, Jonathan and a team of researchers tracked the stories and mental health of a group of middle-aged people over a period of two years. Some were diagnosed with major physical illnesses, such as cancer, during the research period. Jonathan's team observed that the way people told their life stories *before* they got sick "helped to predict their mental health *after* they got sick". A person who could tell an empowering story about their life – featuring positive themes like redemption – was more likely to have higher levels of psychological wellbeing when they became physically ill. This suggests that our stories may help to protect our mental health when life gets tough.

The research in this field is still in its early stages. But a mind-blowing idea has emerged from Jonathan's work: The way we tell our stories could be even more important than whether good or bad things happen to us. In Jonathan's studies, the participants who had the best psychological outcomes didn't necessarily have easy lives, or experience less suffering than other people. However, they had written constructive, meaningful stories about their experiences. The process of authoring your own story doesn't happen automatically, Jonathan says. Each of us must choose to do it. Here's what he told me:

> "The story of your life has an objective impact on your mental health. Being aware of that is really important. 'Hey, I'm not only the main character; I'm also the author.' In my classes, I have plenty of ambitious, high-achieving college students for whom this is a revelation. I remind them, 'You are the storyteller – and playing that role really matters.'"

*

New Zealand has a problem with poverty. Many children go to school without shoes on their feet or food in their stomachs, and we don't expect those kids to thrive, because they don't have the resources to do so. I reckon there's another kind of poverty that can be equally damaging. It's what I call "narrative poverty" – the absence of a healthy story upon which to build your life. Narrative poverty isn't defined by anything like socio-economic status, race or gender. It affects people from all corners of our society. I have met hundreds of adults – including many who appear to be successful – who are living out of sparse stories. Their stories are disjointed. There are huge gaps. Those stories don't seem to be going anywhere. If you don't have a coherent story for your life, the world will gladly write you one for free.

As depression took hold of me, I realised that, although I helped other people to tell their stories, I had paid very little attention to my own. I didn't really know what my story was about. I didn't know what kind of character I was. I didn't know where my plot was taking me. All I knew was that I was stuck, and possibly heading towards a bad ending. But this story was not written by someone else. It was not handed to me. It was not inflicted on me. It was written *by* me. And that meant I didn't need to accept what was already on the page. I had written a draft in pencil, and I had the power to change it. Perhaps my brain wasn't broken, after all. Perhaps my story was broken.

Our stories become our reality.

4. AUTHOR

Getting depressed was like being hit by a car and having to phone the ambulance myself, while I was lying in the middle of the road. Pedestrians were idly walking past, oblivious to how badly I was injured. Once the ambulance arrived, the driver hopped out and handed me the keys. I dragged my battered body into the vehicle and took myself to hospital. There, I showed up at the emergency department, covered in blood and bruises. A doctor asked, "What seems to be the problem, sir?" I had to explain to him, in great detail, exactly what my injuries were, and convince him that they were real. He warmly congratulated me for seeking help. Then he handed me a first-aid kit, left an after-dinner mint on my pillow, and went home.

My metaphor may seem over-the-top, but that's how I felt when I entered the mental health system. I know many others who have had similarly alienating experiences. It takes a lot of courage to admit to a stranger that you're struggling, but we do it because we have been assured that plenty of "help" is available, and that all we need to do is ask for it. That's what the system tells us to do. At the most vulnerable, confusing moments in our lives, public health messaging encourages us to ring helplines or visit our doctors. I believed that if I waved a white flag, someone would ride in on a white horse and carry me to safety.

That's not how it happened. In his 15-minute consultation, my GP didn't have time to conduct a meaningful assessment of my symptoms, and clearly didn't have specialist knowledge of mental health. He told me that I had depression, but he didn't want to put that word into my medical notes in case an employer or insurance provider wanted to read them in the future. (He was trying to protect me, but that added to the sense of shame I was already carrying.) After my visits, I never received a follow-up phone call from the clinic to see how I was doing, or whether I needed further support. If this was my experience, as an educated working professional in Auckland, I can only imagine how tough it is for people who live in tougher circumstances.

Our public health system is stretched to the max, and I have heard horror stories from so many Kiwis who have found it incredibly difficult to access mental health services – and to be *heard*. The health system, like any other institutional framework, carries bias. The quality of service you receive can depend on so many factors, including your age, race, gender and socio-economic status. Access to good mental health care – even in a developed, fair-minded country like New Zealand – can be profoundly inequitable, especially if you live in a region where those services are limited. Public-funded psychologists often have waiting lists that stretch for months. Private healthcare is way too expensive for most people to afford.

But we also need to cut our health professionals some slack, because the treatment of mental distress is not an exact science. There is still so much that we don't know about the human brain. The history of "treating" mental distress is relatively short, and the profession is still working out how to do that in an effective way. Doctors have vastly different views on which treatments are best for their patients. Key decisions – such as when to make a formal diagnosis and when to prescribe medication – can be heavily influenced by the doctor's own worldview, and their relationship with the patient. That's because doctors, just like us, are human.

Let me be clear: I strongly believe in asking for help. It's dangerous to work through mental health issues by yourself. Everyone should have access to high-quality professional support. However, I also believe that in our attempt to encourage people to seek help, we have actually *overstated* the value of the "help" itself. The brutal truth is that asking for help does not necessarily mean you will receive the support you deserve. Your doctor is not a magician, and can't "fix" you. Your survival cannot depend on a public health system that may or may not be able to meet your needs. In fact, that kind of dependence is pretty disempowering. Instead, each of us can take responsibility for our own wellbeing.

That's what I wanted to do. When I got depressed, I spent a lot of time trying to change my behaviours (for example, by exercising, modifying my diet and improving my sleep habits). I also tried to interrupt my negative thought patterns by changing my cognitions (for example, by improving my self-talk, practising mindfulness and focusing on positive messages). I'm pleased that I made these changes, although they didn't make a big difference to my overall state of mind. But when I began to explore the power of storytelling, and discovered the idea that I was the author of my own story, I realised that I had found a new tool to try. If I could regain control of my story, perhaps I could find out whether it was influencing my depression. There was only one place to start: right at the very beginning.

*

I took a deep breath as I walked into a counsellor's office for the first time. I plonked myself down on a blood-red sofa, stared at the tissue box and glass of water beside me, and declared, "I'm here to find my inner child." The counsellor peered at me over his spectacles and said, "Ah." I wasn't sure whether it was more of an "Uh?" or an "Aha!" Nonetheless, he was an expert in inner-child therapy, and was happy to help me find mine. In hindsight, I think I lost my inner child somewhere in Lower Hutt, where I grew up, back in the 1990s. Wherever he was, I hadn't seen or heard from my mini-me for years. But I suspected that he was still in control of my life.

The counsellor and I agreed to explore my earliest memories. I dug into the furthest corners of my mind to see what I could lay my hands on. I was startled by the first memory I retrieved. The year was 1995. It was a crisp, clear, blue-sky day. I was standing at the edge of the school field under a tree, talking to a girl I had a crush on. She said, "Are you brown because you don't shower?" That's it. I can't remember the rest of the conversation. I can't remember what else happened that day. But I can see the sky, smell the grass and remember the feeling of tightness in my five-year-old chest. *Shame*.

Why did that memory come to mind? Why was it stored away in the first place? Perhaps, because it was the very first time I realised I was different.

I plunged back into my mind. It was like a dam had burst, releasing memories that I had been holding for decades. I remembered standing at the edge of the school pool, terrified to get in. I was wearing my new togs and had been ordered by the teacher to jump in the water, like all the other kids. But I had never swum before, and I felt like I was going to drown. *Shame.* I remembered turning up to my first cricket practice and not knowing how to throw or hit a ball like everyone else did. *Shame.* I remembered being bullied for not wearing Reeboks to school. *Shame.* I remembered having to get glasses because I couldn't see properly. I remembered fainting in class during a test, and wetting myself. I remembered being roughed up by the school bully. All of these memories had a common thread: feeling different. Being broken. *Shame, shame, shame.*

*

I was seven when my life changed. A talent scout came to my school to audition kids for a new family game show. The teachers assembled the chattiest, weirdest kids in the library. There, I auditioned – and made the final cut for the studio taping of *Small Talk*. The format was simple. The eccentric host, Jason Gunn, asked adult contestants to predict how nine children would answer a range of obscure questions. (What is a limbo? Can you name a famous actor? Can you impersonate a politician?) I did a very gruff impression of the Leader of the Opposition, Helen Clark. It won me laughs and a hearty round of applause. Jason asked if I ever wanted to become famous. "No," I said matter-of-factly, "because I want to be a normal person."

That was a big fat lie. This was the first moment I received validation – *real* validation – from people who were not part of my family. I had a stage and a captive audience. They listened, laughed and cheered. It felt good. I had already told my parents – at the age of four, apparently – that I wanted to grow up to be a TV reporter. This sealed the deal. In the years that followed, I realised I could perform. I could ask the best questions in class. I could argue and, on a good day, I could even be funny. By performing, I won the affection of my teachers and classmates. All the other stuff I struggled with – feeling different and weird – didn't matter. At least, not when I was in the limelight.

By the age of 13, I decided that it was time to start hustling. I pitched a story about *The Lord of the Rings* movie phenomenon to a prime-time current affairs show called *Holmes*. The producers allowed me to be a guest reporter for one night. Paul Holmes, the legendary presenter, stumbled over the pronunciation of my name on air, and referred to me as a "her" rather than a "he". But I didn't care. I was in business. I started writing for a youth magazine called *Tearaway*, and edited its election coverage. At 15, I rocked up to the top floor of the Beehive to interview Prime Minister Helen Clark – the same woman I had impersonated on that game show many years earlier.

My aspirations kept growing. At 16, with the self-confidence that only a teenager can muster, I started pitching story ideas to national newspapers. I sent my proposals by email, claiming I was a "freelance journalist". Newsrooms, already thin on resources and desperate for copy, began commissioning major features from me, without doing any CV or reference checks, and without even knowing that I was a high-school kid. I was paid $800 for my first piece for *The New Zealand Herald*, a 2000-word investigation into the Ministry of Youth Development. It was quoted by an MP in Parliament's debating chamber. I knew I had found my calling.

By 17, I was in overdrive. I scored my own weekly slot on New Zealand's top morning TV show, *Breakfast*. On Tuesday mornings, I woke up at 5.30 am and took the train to Wellington. A lady called Karen would plaster my face with make-up, and by 7.20 am I was on live TV, offering hot takes on the issues of the day. Then, I'd change into my school uniform in the corridor outside the studio, and take the train to school, walking through the gate just in time for the first period. By age 18, I had interviewed *High School Musical* star Zac Efron in Sydney. I had reported on tsunami relief in the Solomon Islands, and spoken to Kiwi entrepreneurs under the pyramids in Egypt. I had interviewed leading cultural figures, from Archbishop Desmond Tutu to celebrity chef Jamie Oliver.

While I was working, I did a public policy degree in the little spare time I had. But reporting was my real focus. Some of the old hacks in the newsroom made life difficult for me – and I don't really blame them. I turned up out of nowhere, without a journalism qualification. I hadn't spent years earning my stripes by answering phones and running errands, as some of them had. But I also found kind, patient producers who were willing to mentor me. They championed my work, and I started breaking stories. An old lady who was ripped off by a real-estate agent got a house – for free. A youth welfare policy that was splitting up families was scrapped by the government. A man who was about to be deported was allowed to stay in the country. I realised that stories could motivate people to *do* things. They could bring about change.

As my TV career began to take off, I had so much to be proud of. But I never allowed myself to *feel* proud, because I didn't feel worthy of my success. From a young age, I had learnt that I needed to earn my self-worth by performing for others. You may think, *Yeah, that's because he's one of those insecure TV-types*. But I have noticed that almost everyone is performing – hoping to earn favour from other people. People perform in boardrooms, factories, hospitals and classrooms. We perform as colleagues, as parents, as friends. We mistakenly believe that we can use our achievements to prove to others that we are good enough. So, we work harder, run faster and reach higher. Eventually, it becomes impossible to keep performing – and that's when life begins to fall apart.

*

There was one more vivid childhood memory that surfaced during counselling. When I was at primary school, my teacher brought her dog to class each day. The dog was white, fluffy and adorable. He sat patiently on the classroom floor, with his little pink tongue hanging out of his mouth. I was five years old and didn't have a pet at home, so this dog was the coolest thing I had ever seen. As a sensitive, insecure kid, the dog gave me comfort. I would take care of him when the teacher went to the staffroom for morning tea. She left a bowl of water out for him – the little guy was thirsty. When it was time for class, the teacher led the dog into a cupboard behind her desk and shut the door. That seemed weird, but I was only five, so it didn't bother me.

Many years later, as an adult, I realised that I had been duped. There was no dog. It was just a figment of my imagination – and a stroke of genius on my teacher's part. Every day, she held out a bright red leash and told us it was attached to an invisible dog. We just needed to use our imagination to see him. As she began to describe this pretend dog, he materialised in front of us. He became real. And, as the teacher walked around the classroom holding a red leash, a little bit of magic happened in my five-year-old mind. There's a great lesson in this. Stories don't just describe reality – they *become* reality. A simple story is powerful enough to bring something to life, whether it's a dog, an idea or a belief. Not just for five-year-olds, but adults too.

As storytellers, none of us are objective. We have blind spots. We have biases. We don't have the whole picture. But we also don't have to accept the stories that have been presented to us. Over the years, I have interviewed many people who have grasped this important truth – the idea that we are the authors of our own stories, and that we have the power to change them. For some people, that process was life-changing. For others, it was life-saving. I was willing to follow their lead. If I could rewrite my own story, then I could live *into* a new narrative. Perhaps that would allow me to find a way out of my depression.

You're the author.

II.
Rewrite your past

5. TRAUMA

People do crazy things to escape their pain. Some people drink too much. Some smoke. Some gamble. And some become white supremacists. In 2015, I discovered that a group of them had been dropping racist leaflets in letterboxes across the lower North Island. The leaflets said *IMMIGRATION = EBOLA*. It was such a ridiculous connection that it almost seemed comical, but the flyer's creators were deadly serious. The self-described Right Wing Resistance was a fledgling army of wannabe nationalists who were fighting against diversity and multiculturalism. Fearing for the survival of the white race, they wanted to turn New Zealand into a paradise for the pale-skinned. Back then – four years before the Christchurch terror attack – I was curious. Who were these nutters? And did they pose a threat?

In the newsroom, there was much debate about whether I should do the story. Some colleagues argued that it was foolish to give xenophobic hatemongers a national media platform. But I argued that it was important to show the audience that such extreme views existed within our society. I've always believed we can only address our seething underbelly of racism by naming it. So, I tracked down this so-called resistance and paid a visit to one of their rallies in Palmerston North. I found a motley crew of about 20 surly men, decked out in leather jackets, patches and swastika tattoos. They marched through the town square, waving New Zealand flags and chanting about white pride.

As a Sri Lankan Kiwi, I found their behaviour disgusting. But, as I talked to these men, I discovered that their hateful, warped worldviews had an unlikely origin: trauma. Some had endured harmful childhood experiences. Others had struggled with education and employment, and had failed to find their footing in the world. Many of them had negative life experiences that related to people of other cultures. The group's leader told me that his wife left him for an Arab man, and his scrap-metal business was suffering after much of his work went to the Chinese market. Of course, none of this excused his group's vile, inflammatory, delusional behaviour. Racism is racism, full stop. But understanding these men's histories gave me some context about why they were intent on attacking other people.

Behind their bravado, many of the men were carrying deep pain, anger and hurt that may never have been expressed, let alone worked through. Some were grieving. Many were lonely. And they were trying to deal with their pain by passing it on to people of colour. When I told this story on TV, I showed the men for what they were, and they didn't look pretty. But I also wanted to explain that some of them were emotionally broken. After the programme, I had a call from a member of the "resistance". He said, "I just wanted to let you know, after the way you treated us, I've realised that there are some good ones out there." "Good what?" I asked. "Brown people," he replied.

*

Trauma is the Greek word for "wound". In modern psychology, trauma represents the brain's response to distressing events. For many of us, our earliest traumatic experiences took place during childhood. Some kids were neglected – not only physically, but also emotionally. Some watched their families get torn apart. Some were exposed to crime, dysfunction and illness. A vast body of research has shown that these adverse experiences can have a toxic effect on the brain. Trauma can affect our ability to process emotions, deal with stress and respond to other forms of adversity. It can have a profound effect on how we engage with the world.

The problem is, Kiwi culture encourages us to keep silent about the things that have hurt us. Throughout history, whole generations have been denied the opportunity to speak about their trauma. Those stories have been suppressed because of colonisation, sexism, cultural oppression, economic power and many other factors. Put simply, if someone's story does not line up with the story of the dominant culture, it usually gets squashed. But silence has a corrosive effect. If we can't give voice to our trauma, it often finds other ways to express itself, through dysfunctional behaviour – including violence and substance abuse – or unhealthy relationships.

Some of us choose to stay silent about our pain, and try to distract ourselves from our unwanted emotions. *Eat a burger. Play another game. Have another coffee. Stay in bed. Skip the gym session. Scroll through Facebook. Buy some clothes. Have a beer.* These decisions feel good in the moment, and they can help us to get rid of those gnarly feelings. But burying negative emotions is a bit like sending rubbish to a landfill. The stuff you bury doesn't break down, doesn't become smaller, and doesn't go away. It's just out of sight. Those emotions continue to interfere with our day-to-day lives, and can affect our wellbeing.

When mental distress shows up, we can choose to view it as an invitation – perhaps the greatest invitation some of us will ever receive. It's a chance to begin the process of undoing the silence that has been forced upon us – or the silence that we have chosen. If we can examine the events in our past, we can identify the harmful narratives that we created about those events and start to rewrite them. Rewriting is not about airbrushing bad things out, or making unicorns pop up in the middle of the story. It's about taking a step back and asking, "Is there another way of looking at what happened? Is this story helping or hurting me? Is there a more useful way of telling it?"

*

Karina Andrews was nervous. She paced up and down the footpath. Took a drag on her cigarette. Paced again. We were about to film a story in Hobsonville Point, a former Royal New Zealand Air Force base in West Auckland. Karina grew up there in the 1970s, while her dad was in the air force. By the time we visited, the old base had been replaced by rows of overpriced cookie-cutter apartments. Only a few relics from the air force era remained, including a set of large aircraft hangars with broken windows and cracked facades. For many of us, a visit to our childhood neighbourhood would bring back fond memories. For Karina, it was incredibly painful. In Hobsonville, she was sexually abused by her own dad.

> "He always said, 'Don't tell Mummy I did this with your clothes off.' It was our secret. It wasn't for anybody else to know. I was six years old. I didn't know any better. I didn't know it was wrong. He said, 'If people knew what I was doing, they would take you away from the family.' I felt like it was my fault, so I wasn't going to tell anybody."

Karina was a timid child, a bookworm who rarely got into mischief. She didn't go out of her way to make new friends, and she didn't venture far from the family home. That's partly because her father, Robert Roper, was a "domineering presence". He sexually abused his daughter for about a decade, until she was 17 years old. Karina didn't feel safe enough to tell anyone about her abuse, even after she left home and became an adult. By then, she was partying heavily, and using drugs and alcohol to blank out the memories of what her father had done to her. She had "completely lost respect" for her own body, and chose to work in a strip club, because she believed that was the only way to earn people's attention and affection.

> "I was receiving love if I was receiving sex. If a man wanted to have sex with me, I thought he loved me. I craved that. I really craved that. I was worth nothing. I was always drunk. I had no self-esteem. I had been little more than a sexual plaything for a predator, and that was it. That's honestly how I saw myself, and for years, I didn't know who I was."

Eventually, Karina got married and had a family of her own. But her childhood abuse continued to haunt her. In 2012, she began having flashbacks that reminded her of the brutality of that abuse. Over the course of a fortnight, she became quieter and quieter. She struggled to cook a meal or pick her son up from school. In fact, she couldn't even leave the house. One day, she went "ballistic". Karina raced to the garage, grabbed a claw hammer and tried to hit herself. Her husband, Paul, wrestled the hammer off her, and restrained her while phoning the police. Karina was put into a mental health unit. There, she made the incredible decision to release the secret she had kept for almost 30 years. She would press charges against her father, and wouldn't stop "until he was held accountable".

The #MeToo movement had not yet hit the headlines when Karina stood up in the Auckland District Court in 2014. Her dad was in the same room. When she made eye contact with him, Karina didn't feel scared. She just saw an old man "whose past had finally caught up with him". And she wasn't the only one to testify. Four other women told the court that Robert Roper had offended against them. He was found guilty on 20 charges including rape and sexual assault. The women were euphoric. After the verdict, they walked to a nearby Irish pub to celebrate. (It was called The Fiddler, Karina noted dryly.) There, she laughed, drank and closed the book on one of the toughest days of her life: the day she sent her own father to jail.

Six years on, Karina is still triggered by things that bring back memories of her abuse – like the smell of Old Spice. But the way she talks about her trauma has changed dramatically. She understands that the abuse was not her fault. She no longer describes herself as a victim; instead, she prefers to be known as a survivor. And her self-worth is no longer tied to her father's actions. Now, it comes from helping other people. On Mondays, Karina fills a crockpot with meat and vegetables and drops it off to Rotorua's homeless community, and chats with people about the ups and downs of life. She volunteers in a rest home, where she does arts and crafts with dementia patients. And she supports other survivors of sexual abuse. It's a remarkable transformation for a woman who was once too scared to leave her own house.

> "I was heading towards an early grave, so I had to change my story. Once you put your feet on that path, you walk it alone. Having said that, I'm not special. I'm a very normal woman. There is nothing remarkable about me, other than the fact that I was willing to do the work on myself."

*

In recent years, the "origin stories" of our favourite superheroes have become more popular than ever. The film industry has tapped into a goldmine by exploring these backstories, and they often share a common theme: childhood adversity. Spider-Man was a lonely orphan who was bitten by a radioactive spider. Superman was sent to Earth by his parents, who were saving him from the destruction of Planet Krypton. Batman was just a youngster when he watched his parents get murdered. Origin stories give depth to these characters and provide context by explaining how their early experiences influenced their development.

There is power in real-life origin stories too. In social services, "trauma-informed care" is a growing movement that aims to shift the focus from "What's wrong with this person?" to "What *happened* to this person?" Advocates of trauma-informed care recognise that mental distress, learning difficulties and problematic behaviour are often the symptoms of underlying trauma. In prisons, schools and hospitals, the power of storytelling can be used to help people unearth the narratives that are influencing their thoughts and actions. If someone can identify their trauma, they can begin to explore its impact on their life. The good news is that a story is not doomed just because it had a bad beginning.

I went to counselling because I wanted to discover my own origin story. I embarked on a months-long process to school up on my personal history. I read my school reports. I went through photo albums. I had conversations with my parents. I re-read my journal. Through that process, I identified three key trauma-driven narratives that had begun to take shape during my childhood. Firstly, that my body was defective and would always let me down. Secondly, that I was no one's priority. (Despite having a loving, nurturing family, I felt rejected by my peers.) Thirdly, that I would never be good enough for someone else. As I grew into an adult, I felt unworthy and unlovable.

Those narrative strands were rooted in my childhood experiences: being bullied, feeling different, and growing up in a migrant family in New Zealand. I was straddling two cultural worlds. As one of the only ethnic kids in my school, I was ashamed of my Sri Lankan culture, and my parents didn't look or talk like other kids' parents. I thought there was something wrong with me. As I grew up, I built my entire life upon the story that five-year-old Jehan had drawn in crayon. That story – about a scared, vulnerable kid who was afraid of getting hurt – helped to protect me as a child, but served me poorly as an adult. It turned me into a workaholic. It made me reluctant to go on dates. It prevented me from taking risks. That story was suffocating and, I was pretty sure, a significant factor in my depression.

People often say that you can't rewrite history. But I thought, *Of course I can – I'm the one who wrote it in the first place.* I began to shape new narratives around my childhood memories. I could choose to have empathy for the girl who asked me if I was brown because I didn't shower. She was five years old and didn't know any better. I could have empathy for the boy who bullied me the most because I knew that he was a victim of childhood abuse. I could have empathy for my parents, who had escaped a civil war and moved to the other side of the world. In a new country, they did the very best they could, and gave me a safe, loving home. And, most importantly, I could have empathy for myself. I was just a shy, sensitive kid who was trying to earn his place in the world.

The source of your pain lies in your past.

6. SCARS

The quest for perfection has never been more exhausting. In the digital age, each of us can craft and control our public image. From arty profile pics to dreamy holiday snaps, our social media pages act as billboards, displaying idealised (and unrealistic) versions of ourselves. But, when we are naked and alone, we can't hide behind the soft glow of an Instagram filter – and it's hard to ignore our flaws. On our bodies, scars provide physical maps of our most painful experiences. I have met people who carry scars from explosions, surgeries, pregnancies, self-harm and accidents. When the skin is injured, the body places a mark there, as if to say, "Something important happened here. Don't forget that you were hurt."

I'm grateful that I wasn't physically hurt during my childhood, but I do bear emotional scars. The bullying I experienced left a huge dent in my confidence. I struggled to make friends, and had no sense of belonging. I became self-critical and, often, self-loathing. But no one knew how much I was struggling to accept myself because I learnt to cover up my pain. As I grew into my teens, I developed an unhealthy obsession with my image. There wasn't anything wrong with my body, but it came to represent everything I didn't like about myself.

At 56 kilos, I punched well below my weight. People often told me that being skinny was a First World problem. "Oh, poor you," they would say, rolling their eyes. "You get to eat whatever you like." I knew many women would have killed for my figure, but, while thin girls are admired, thin guys are looked upon with deep suspicion. ("Don't you eat? Don't you play sport? Have you been ill?") In our culture, to be male and slim is to be weak, vulnerable, effeminate. Our national mythology tells us that New Zealand was built by stocky farmers, rugby players, adventurers and hunter-gatherers. If you're a man and it's possible to drive a bus through your thigh gap, there's something wrong with you.

I hated what I saw in the mirror. When I inhaled, I could see my own ribcage. My shoulder blades stuck out like little fins on my back. My biceps were barely bigger than my wrists. I often wore two singlets underneath my T-shirt to make my torso look broader. Sometimes I even bought clothes made for 12-year-old boys, because most menswear was too big for me. By my late teens, I embarked on a quest to "fix" my body. I spent thousands on gym fees and personal trainers. I changed my diet to increase my calorie intake, and forced myself to eat even when I was full. I guzzled protein shakes and popped expensive supplements. I did sit-ups in my bedroom, to the point that one day I passed out and woke up on the floor. I was just glad that I hadn't fallen through the cracks.

*

It probably seems odd that someone who was so self-conscious about his body chose one of the most image-obsessed jobs out there: being a TV reporter. On *Seven Sharp*, my weight became a running gag. I was put into physically demanding situations that were likely to produce comedic results, like doing the police's gruelling fitness test and being tackled on live TV by a rugby player. "Have you *seen* Jehan? He's a stick," exclaimed Mike Hosking during a segment on Men's Health Week. It was good-natured banter, and I helped to feed it. But I was surprised when strangers offered unsolicited opinions about my physique. I saw tweets like this one: *Spotted @jehancasinader at Wellington Airport. Would someone please get that man a nice big steak? He's so much leaner in real life.*

In moments like this, I felt my childhood scars swelling beneath my skin and threatening to break open. Those emotional scars ran deep. Even though I had grown into an adult, the scars hadn't faded; they were just hidden. No matter how much success I experienced in my career, it was tainted by the narrative that my body was defective and, no matter how hard I tried, it would always hold me back. Although no one could see the chinks in my armour, I knew that I was damaged. In front of a camera, I felt more exposed than ever.

*

Years later, I was given the chance to co-host a week of *Breakfast* – the same show I was once a panellist on as a teenager. On my first day of presenting duties, I crawled out of bed at 3.30 am, and climbed into the clothes I had laid out the night before. I drove to work, pumped coffee into my veins, and stared at my computer for an hour, overwhelmed by the amount of information that would pass through my brain during the live three-hour show. After make-up (a light dusting of cocoa powder, or something like it) I walked into the studio, pushed back my shoulders and lifted my stool as high as it could go. But I was about to interview someone who would challenge my obsession with body image: a young man who wore his own story on his skin.

Joshua Sade-Inia was born into a family that couldn't look after him, and he was taken into state care at the age of two. In the years that followed, he passed through more than ten foster homes across the North Island. Some of those were good homes, but many were places of darkness. Joshua says he experienced physical, mental and sexual abuse. His life was regularly upended, as he was forced to move towns and schools. He was severely bullied, struggled with his sense of self-worth, and believed that he was destined to be a failure. Joshua's story is shamefully common. As a Māori boy, he believed the state care system had written him off before he even had a chance to build a life.

> "As a kid, I hoped that I could live under a bridge one day. That was the extent of my hope. I just couldn't expect any more than that, because of my circumstances. By my teens, I was self-harming as a way to try to cope with my pain. I was angry, sad and resentful, but I kept bottling up all those emotions. Eventually, the cap on the bottle exploded."

On a beautiful Sunday morning, Joshua was overwhelmed by his pain and "just wanted out". He grabbed a lighter from the kitchen, found a can of petrol in the garage, and decided to set himself on fire. After pouring petrol over his body, he stood outside his foster-parents' house for ten minutes, thinking about his existence. He dwelt on how much he hated the world. He wanted to bring his pain to an end. The lighter in his hand was almost empty, but it spat out a single spark – and that's all it took. Joshua's body went up in flames. First came the heat; suffocating and intense. Then came the agony. Joshua screamed until there was nothing coming out of his mouth.

He tried to take off his T-shirt but kept getting caught inside it. The flames were wrapping around his windpipe and climbing towards his head. Joshua ran towards the house, trying to run away from the fire. ("Turns out you can't really do that," he told me.) His foster-dad was standing at the back door. He pushed Joshua over and rolled him around on the wet grass. But, because Joshua's body was so hot, the fire reignited. Eventually, once the flames were out, his foster-parents put water on his burns, while waiting for an ambulance to arrive. On the way to hospital, a remarkable thing happened: Joshua's attitude to life changed completely.

"I thought, *I've made such a big mistake.* I said to the ambulance officers, 'I don't want to die. Please don't let me die.' They said, 'We're going to do everything we can.' That wasn't enough for me. I thought, *Oh my gosh, there's still a chance that I'm going to die.* I was in shock, so I was coming in and out of consciousness. That's when they put me into an induced coma."

When he came out of the coma a few days later, Joshua was covered in bandages. He had survived burns to almost half his body. When it was time to remove the dressings, he vividly remembers a doctor unwrapping his left hand. The moment he saw his scars for the first time, Joshua's whole perception of his body changed. He thought he looked like "a monster who would be disfigured for life". For three years, he had to wear pressure garments. He did physio to recover his range of movement, and he had more than a dozen surgeries and skin grafts. Almost a decade after his suicide attempt, Joshua is still under medical care. As a 22-year-old who is open to dating, he often feels self-conscious about his skin. But his relationship with his body is changing.

"It has taken years for me to come to terms with my scars, and it's a continuous learning process. But now I see beauty in them. They don't have to be defined by negativity. They can actually be a symbol of hope for those who are struggling or going through hard times. My scars show what I have overcome. They tell the story of my resilience."

Joshua is surprised by how many people ask about how he got hurt. He's always willing to share the story, even with complete strangers, because "you never know who will be inspired or helped by it". Now, that story is heading in a new direction. Joshua has begun to explore his whakapapa; his Māori heritage. It's a special process because he couldn't connect with his culture when he was in the foster care system. He is studying law, politics and international relations at Auckland University, and plans to go into politics one day, in the hope of influencing the lives of our most vulnerable people. Joshua wants to be a role model for other young Māori, especially those who have survived abuse in state care.

"If I was given the opportunity to change what I have been through and take back the heartache I have experienced, I wouldn't change any of it. Now that I'm an adult, I don't see my childhood as something to be ashamed of. I want to accept it. I've grown, I've learnt valuable life skills, and it has given me the ambition to make a difference in our society."

*

When I meet a new person, I often ask, "How do you spend your time?" or "What do you do for a living?" Instead, I wish I could say, "Can you show me where you've been hurt?" The fastest way to forge a genuine connection with someone is to understand how they have been wounded. Of course, you can't expect a person to bare their soul the first time you meet them. But you can challenge *yourself* to be vulnerable. I have opened the door to many rich conversations by sharing a small piece of information that reflects my own challenges. By doing so, I tell the other person, "Hey, I'm a bit broken and a bit messed up – and it's okay if you are too."

I came to understand that having scars doesn't make my story invalid. In fact, those scars are part of the story. By carefully exposing them to the light, I have learnt how to become comfortable with showing them to other people. At first, I began talking with my friends about the childhood events that had shaped me. I told my parents about some of the things that I had struggled with. Eventually, I felt confident enough to share my experiences in the media. In recent years, I have spoken openly about my struggles with my body. To my surprise, guys have come up to me on the street and thanked me for showing them that it's okay to talk about how they feel about their image.

Being vulnerable can be really hard. It takes practice and patience. There are times when I still feel ashamed of my emotional scars. But, now that I have learnt to display them, they have far less power over me. In fact, on a good day, I can share Joshua's outlook and see beauty in the areas that usually make me feel broken. I know that I can use my scars to encourage other people to accept their own. And that makes me feel like I'm not as damaged as I once thought.

*

During the Holocaust, Nazi guards printed identification numbers on the forearms of Jewish prisoners. For those who survived the concentration camps, these crude, lopsided marks have provided lifelong physical reminders of the horrors they endured. After the war ended, some survivors tried to surgically remove the markings or cover them up. But in recent decades, many have chosen to openly display their identification numbers and to speak publicly about the stories behind them. These survivors are desperate for the world to remember what happened in camps like Auschwitz-Birkenau. Their fading scars represent one of the darkest periods in history.

Many Holocaust survivors have already passed away. Those who remain are in their eighties and nineties – but their children and grandchildren don't want their incredible stories to be forgotten. Some of the survivors' descendants have chosen to get tattoos that match the inscriptions on their loved ones' arms. It's their way of keeping their parents' and grandparents' legacies alive. By choosing to get tattoos of the Nazi ID numbers, the younger generation is reclaiming the scars of genocide, and turning those scars into a new story that can bring light into the world.

We can all choose to interpret our scars in a positive way, even while experiencing mental distress. We can build good stories around them – stories that tell us more about courage than defeat; more about strength than weakness. As I learnt to be more open about my childhood experiences, I became more confident to go out into the world and say, "This is who I am. This is what happened to me. And this is how it changed me." It didn't make me less depressed, but it allowed me to find some meaning in my most painful experiences. In many ways, my scars are the tattoos that I never asked for.

Scars are part of the story.

7. SCRIPTS

I'll admit it. News reporters talk in a bizarre way. The nasal tone, the strange inflections, the sing-song rhythm. I don't know where it came from, but most reporters adopt that familiar style. Sometimes, it even seems like we're speaking a different language. A storm is a "weather bomb!" or a "wintry blast!" When petrol prices go up, there's "more pain at the pump!" If the roads are busy, it's "commuter chaos!" No one teaches journalists to talk like this. We just pick up the lingo from each other. On camera, I find it easy to slip into the well-established language of news – even if it does sound like I'm having a brain aneurysm.

When there's a lot of information to remember, it's hard to stick to a script. While studio-based presenters can rely on an autocue to feed them their lines, reporters in the field are forced to wing it. We memorise facts and figures, hoping to recall them when the red light comes on. That's always a gamble. One night, I was standing in the rose garden outside Parliament, about to do a live cross on *1 News* at 6 pm. I was feeling confident about the story – an investigation I had worked on for weeks – so I put my notebook down on the grass. I heard the theme music playing in my earpiece, and felt my heart rate kick up a notch as the director counted down: "Standby, Jehan. Ten seconds until we're coming to you ... Five seconds ... And cue!"

At that moment, in front of 600,000 people, my mind went completely blank. I knew I had to relay comments made by a senior government minister, but I couldn't remember them. Words started coming out of my mouth – words that were not even true. I fumbled my way to the end of the segment and handed over to the presenter. I stood in my spot, dazed and confused. *What had I just said? What was going to happen?* The cameraman, Phil, sensed my panic, and smiled as he packed down his lights. "What are you having for lunch tomorrow?" he asked. It was Christmas Eve. Hopefully, the minister hadn't watched my disastrous performance. Given that my phone never rang, I'm pretty sure he was already prepping the ham.

*

Our culture is full of scripts that tell us how to act in the world. We play the roles that we think we're meant to play, and deliver the lines that our parents, teachers and employers have written for us. In New Zealand, the most popular script goes something like this: Leave school, go to university, get a job, get married, work hard, buy a house, provide for your partner and kids, pay your taxes, watch some sport, and have a few decent holidays along the way. If you follow the script correctly for 65 years, you'll have enough money to quit your job and buy some golf clubs. But, in the meantime, you're not meant to scream, cry or yell – unless you've had a few drinks.

Cultural scripts exist for three reasons. Firstly, they work. They've been tried and tested over many decades. Secondly, they're familiar. We've seen our friends and family follow these scripts. Thirdly, they're convenient. Life can be pretty simple when you're meeting society's expectations. You fit in with the crowd and don't have to explain yourself. You just follow the script and trust that it will help you to lead a good, moral life. For many people, life unfolds exactly as expected. Nice family, nice car, nice job. It might seem like they're just going through the motions, but they're happy enough, because they got what they believed they were promised. For others, life takes a turn. Cancer shows up. A marriage falls apart. A house catches fire. A baby is stillborn. The story begins to fall apart – and it's no longer possible to follow the script.

When I became depressed, I felt angry, confused and cheated. I thought, *I didn't sign up for this. This is not how my story was supposed to go.* But I wanted to be like everyone else, so I forced myself to act. I was in a coveted job and was determined to succeed, so I made myself perform at work. When I met new people, I wanted to win them over, so I was performing in my conversations. Living in Auckland, in the affluent suburb of Grey Lynn, I wanted to dress, talk and live in a way that seemed effortless, so I was even performing when I went to the supermarket. Trying to meet people's expectations was draining, but there was no other way to live. Was there?

*

In New Zealand, there's no script more powerful than the All Blacks script. Many boys grow up believing that they're destined to wear the hallowed jersey. When 20-year-old Zac Guildford walked onto the field in Cardiff, Wales, for his first test match as an All Black, he felt the weight of the nation on his shoulders. Zac had grown up in a rugby-obsessed Hawke's Bay family, and he'd always dreamt of playing professionally. But he hadn't anticipated the demands that came with the All Blacks lifestyle. Passing, kicking and scoring are only some of the skills required of modern players. They must also take part in advertising, show up at promotional events, do charity work and act as global ambassadors for their country. As the youngest player in the squad – and barely out of high school – Zac was not prepared for any of that.

> "It was a shock. Ninety per cent of your life as an All Black is scripted. 'This is how you act in public. This is what you can do. This is what you can't say in front of the media. This is how you play.' There was room for my own instinct and flair on the field, but once I was off the field, I was back into script mode. Most All Blacks can adapt to that lifestyle, but with so much stuff going on in my head, I couldn't do that."

Five months earlier, before the whole country knew his name, Zac played in the final of the World Rugby Under 20 Championship in Japan. The Kiwis thrashed the Poms, winning 44–28. When the final whistle blew, Zac was elated. His eyes drifted to the stands, where his parents had been watching the game. There, a bunch of people were standing around his dad, Robert, who had had a heart attack during the game and died before Zac could reach him. Robert, who had played provincial rugby in his younger days, was his son's hero. The tragedy rocked Zac to his core – and it also made him hungrier for greatness. When he was named in the All Blacks squad, he felt a "huge sense of relief", and he knew that his old man would have been proud.

And yet, he couldn't enjoy his newfound glory. Inside his head, he was being battered by grief. Alcohol helped to numb the pain of losing his dad, but it didn't take long for that strategy to fail in a very public way. In 2011, while in Rarotonga for a friend's wedding, Zac staggered into a bar, naked, bleeding and blind drunk. He punched two patrons. The booze-fuelled blowout made world headlines, and the public's reaction was swift and brutal. Zac was vilified for staining the black jersey and letting down his teammates and fans. Sports commentators – as quick to build up a "rising star" as they are to tear that star down when they fail – wrote off his career after he was dropped from the squad. Almost every newspaper adopted a phrase containing six barbed words: "Troubled former All Black Zac Guildford".

But Zac was determined to salvage his career. In 2013, the rugby union held a press conference in Wellington, giving him a chance to make amends. I sat in that room and watched Zac offer a fulsome apology for his mistakes. He admitted that he had a problem with alcohol. The union had sent him to rehab, and his contract had been reinstated. With this lifeline, Zac could have become New Zealand rugby's greatest comeback kid. But, in the following years, he was still hooked – not just by alcohol, but also by drugs and gambling. Despite a series of attempts to get his life back on track, and many public appeals for forgiveness, he continued to make bad decisions. After being dropped from the All Blacks, he played short stints with other clubs, but often didn't last a season. Reflecting on those years, Zac told me:

> "Beneath all the macho-ness of rugby, there was a little boy who just didn't know what to do with life. His anger was bubbling away. He was grieving for his dad. He was scared, nervous, shy, wanting encouragement from male role models. He had a real lack of confidence. No matter how hard I tried and how much I achieved, it was always like, 'Am I there yet?' Even when I reached the heights of becoming an All Black, it never really felt enough."

A year ago, Zac began taking part in group therapy with other men. In the room with those guys, he felt safe enough to open up, knowing that he wouldn't be judged. Through therapy, Zac discovered that his addictions, depression and anxiety were the manifestations of his inner turmoil. As a boy, he never learnt to process or articulate his emotions. Although his dad was an excellent role model, he wasn't big on communication. Zac spent years trying to live up to Robert's expectations, but "never really knew what those expectations were". Now, he recognises that he can write a different script for his life – one that allows him to express himself in an authentic way.

Journalists usually hate interviewing rugby players. On the field they perform magic, but in front of a camera they seize up. Most players gaze at their shoes while muttering their favourite phrase: "Yeah, nah." But Zac is different. He's known for being sensitive, thoughtful and honest. As I have interviewed him over the years, I have watched him become more willing to be vulnerable. No longer shackled to the stoic All Blacks script, he can expand his focus beyond rugby. He has been working as a teacher aide, helping children who need encouragement in the classroom. While rugby is still an important part of Zac's life, he is finally content to be himself. He hopes his dad would have been just as proud of his new way of life.

> "Dad's death will always hurt. But now I'm able
> to take off my mask and let everyone know who
> I am and how I feel. I've learnt to forgive myself

and make peace with most of the mistakes I made. Back then, every time I screwed up, it was like having to climb Mount Everest. I'd climb all the way up the mountain, and then go right back down again. But now, when I make a mistake, it's just a speed bump in the road."

*

While growing up, I was obsessed with how *unlike* everyone else I thought I was. I was useless at sport. I didn't have a PlayStation. I didn't listen to Eminem. I didn't drink. I had no interest in getting my driver's licence. I didn't even have a Facebook profile. I didn't think I needed any of this stuff in my life. There were other things that were more important to me – incredibly nerdy things, like leading the school debating team and being on the school board. When my fledgling journalism career began during my teens, I started receiving opportunities that were beyond my wildest dreams – but I still felt like I was failing, because I wasn't living a typical teenage life.

At age 18, Disney offered to fly me to New York to interview a new band called The Jonas Brothers. They had shot a made-for-TV movie, *Camp Rock*, and were planning a red-carpet premiere. There was a catch: I needed to get on a plane just 48 hours later. Disney took care of everything. The company flew me business class to New York, by myself. A limo picked me up from LaGuardia Airport, and drove me to the Hilton on Sixth Avenue. It was the kind of glitzy junket that any journo would dream of. But I remember what it felt like to wake up in New York on my first morning in the city. I opened the curtains, and there was that famous skyline. I couldn't enjoy the moment. All I remember thinking is, *Why can't I be like everyone else?*

I have felt the same on many other assignments. Like when I sat in a boat travelling down the Nile in Egypt at sunset. Or when I was zip-lining through a forest in Whistler, Canada. Or when I was sitting in the rooftop bar of a Hong Kong hotel. I have worked with incredible camera operators and producers over the years, but I have also spent a lot of time by myself – on planes, in hotels and in front of computer screens. The most productive periods of my career have often been marked by a deep sense of isolation – a feeling that I was out of step with people my own age. That has often prevented me from enjoying the good things in front of me.

As depression took hold, I became painfully aware that I hadn't followed the life course that many of my friends were choosing – going travelling, getting married, having families and buying houses. Instead, I had put almost all my energy into my work, with a degree of focus that many people don't have until their thirties or forties. That didn't mean I was a failure. It meant I had written a script for my life that reflected my own values at the time. It brought me many rich, meaningful experiences. I still really wanted all those other things too. I just hadn't found them yet.

The dominant scripts in our culture can be really helpful. They can guide us through the chaos of modern life. They can show us what is possible, and give us things to hope for and aspire to. But they can also have a catastrophic impact on our mental health. Cultural scripts don't work for everyone. Not all of us can reach the milestones that society expects us to reach – in the right order, and at the right speed. Life presents us with positive opportunities, as well as messy, painful situations, often when we least expect them. Rather than trying to follow popular narratives, I came to understand that I could write my own script.

*

Remember the 1998 movie *The Truman Show*? Jim Carrey, at the peak of his powers, played Truman Burbank, an ordinary, hapless resident of a seaside town called Seahaven Island. An insurance broker by day, Truman has a dreamy suburban existence – until he works out that he has been born into a reality-TV freak show. He has spent his whole life in an artificial world, built on a film set. Truman is on camera 24 hours a day, surrounded by actors who are, unbeknown to him, assigned to play roles in his life, including his wife. From the day of his birth, Truman's every move has been broadcast live. The world is transfixed, but his life – all of it – has been a lie. He has no idea what lies outside his fictional universe, and no idea how to escape.

Despite this, Truman makes the brave decision to try to break out of the tedious story that has been manufactured for him. He steals a boat and sails through a storm to the edge of the TV studio, crashing into a solid wall that has clouds and water painted on it. There, Truman finds a set of stairs leading to a door that opens out onto the real world. The movie ends with him stepping through that door – an act of courage. But what is most extraordinary is that the door has been available to Truman his whole life. The producers can't keep him in that studio against his will. He has *always* been able to leave. It is only when his life becomes unbearable that Truman decides to stop following the script and seek true freedom. He just has to want it – and choose it.

Stop following the script.

III. Reinvent your character

8. IDENTITY

The red carpet had been rolled out, and the champagne was on ice. In November 2018, I arrived at the New Zealand Television Awards without knowing that it would be one of the most significant nights of my career. As I sat in the audience, surrounded by many of my childhood TV heroes, I heard the words, "Reporter of the Year", and then my own name. At just 28 years old, I was gobsmacked. I walked up to the stage to accept my award. It was a special moment, but I felt like a fraud. As I stepped up to the microphone, I desperately wanted to tell the truth: I was at the bottom of a very deep hole. After almost three years of mental distress, my suicidal thoughts had become unrelenting. Every day, I was caught in an all-consuming battle to control my state of mind.

In my quest to improve my mental health, I had left no stone unturned. I had done two years of counselling.

I went for a run most days. I tried breathing exercises. I bought a mindfulness colouring book designed for adults. And yet, there was still a gaping hole in my soul. But, as I stood at the podium in Auckland's Civic Theatre, I couldn't say that. Instead, I made a rambling speech about the stories I had worked on. I thanked my colleagues. I affirmed the value of good journalism. Then I stepped off the stage, holding my Perspex trophy. A cold glass of bubbles was thrust into my hand as I was pushed in front of a photographer's lens. In the media, this is what success is supposed to look like: glamorous and intoxicating. But mainly, I just felt wrecked.

My distress had become a constant part of my life – a kind of background noise that was always present, no matter how hard I tried to drown it out. Some days, it sounded like a low hum of static. But most days, the volume was turned all the way up. At my worst moments, my suicidal thoughts felt overwhelming. I didn't really want to kill myself. I just wanted the pain to stop. But I was increasingly convinced that if I didn't get better, I would end up taking my life. Some nights, I would get in my car and drive over the Auckland Harbour Bridge. I would head north, then further north – nowhere in particular. In the darkness on State Highway One, I would put my foot on the pedal, grip the steering wheel, and scream.

IDENTITY

*

What happens to a depressed person when you plonk them into the Mediterranean Sea? I was keen to find out. When my best friend, Tommy, and his wife, Brooke, travelled to Europe for a long holiday, I forced myself to join them for a ten-day jaunt around Italy. It was the middle of summer, a year before Covid-19 ravaged the country. In Naples, we were surrounded by beautiful Italians riding Vespas, with their pristine leather bags slung over their shoulders. This truly was *la dolce vita*. For days, we gorged ourselves on gelato, antipasto, espresso, prosecco and all the other magical Italian treats that end in the letter O. But, as I immersed myself in Italy's delights, I couldn't escape the fact that I was depresso.

I had hoped that my trip to Italy would provide a holiday from my mental distress, but my depression just followed me to the other side of the world. By the time we reached the glittering Amalfi Coast, I was really struggling. At our rented beachfront villa, I lay on a deckchair, gazing past the rugged coastline and into the ocean. For two hours, tears streamed down my face. *What's wrong with me? How is it possible that I'm in such a beautiful place, with people I love, but I can't appreciate it?* I couldn't understand what had happened to the person I used to be – a person who would have soaked up all the goodness that surrounded him.

Before depression, I'd had a childlike sense of wonder. Even as an adult, I was easily excited by simple pleasures like taking a warm cake out of the oven, collecting pine cones in a forest, or watching a bird build its nest. These ordinary experiences brought me joy, and reminded me of the vast beauty of the material world. I bought Christmas lights from The Warehouse and kept them strung up around my flat's living room all year round. To me, the world was a sparkly place, and I chased every glimmer of light that caught my eye. My curiosity fuelled my working life too. It helped me to construct a powerful identity for myself as a journalist. I was a storyteller. I was a listener. I was a traveller. I was an investigator. I was able to solve problems, and introduce people to new ideas.

In my mid-twenties, depression stole that identity and presented me with a new costume – one that didn't fit properly. It was hot and heavy, and I could barely move around in it, but I felt like I had to wear it. I wasn't enjoying my work. I didn't care as deeply about the stories I was telling. The lifestyle that once brought me satisfaction – travelling, talking and tweeting – felt meaningless. I struggled to answer the phone. I felt distant from my friends and family. Bit by bit, depression dismantled the framework that held me together. My mental distress wasn't just part of my identity; it became my *only* identity. This was the character I thought I would have to play for the rest of my life.

By the time I travelled to Italy, my world had become incredibly dark. I wasn't holidaying as an ordinary tourist – I was a depressed tourist, and no amount of gelato could change that. On a countryside estate in rural Tuscany, I lay next to a pool, quietly seething. I was angry at the world, angry at myself, and angry at the loud, obnoxious American kid who was ruining the serenity by screeching and splashing in the water. I remembered what it was like to see the world as a child does: wide open and full of possibilities. What would it take to become like a child again? What would it take to reclaim the identity that depression had taken from me?

*

When Liam Malone looked down at his legs, he knew exactly how the world saw him: as "a disabled kid". Liam was born with missing fibula bones in both of his legs. When he was 18 months old, his parents made the heartbreaking decision to amputate his legs below the knee. He grew up with prosthetics, which had a profound effect on how he viewed himself, and on what he thought he was capable of. At school, Liam says he "failed" in every physical competition he participated in, from swimming to running. Even his academic performance was hampered by a deep lack of confidence. Sometimes, his dad found him crying in his room. Liam couldn't understand why he wasn't allowed to have "real legs" like all the other kids at school.

> "Society labelled me as 'disabled', and that's how I viewed myself. It's just so debilitating for a child's optimism. I was very lucky because of how great my parents were – I won the lottery in that sense. They just pushed me, and pushed me, and pushed me. Having artificial legs was never an excuse. But I remember my friends' parents saying, 'Life's so unfair on you, having artificial legs. Life's so unfair.'"

Puberty is an awkward time for any kid, but it was especially difficult for Liam. At intermediate school, he was teased a lot, and decided to fight back by becoming one of the school bullies. He hassled his classmates, mocking any aspect of their appearance that he could seize upon. That gave him a temporary sense of power, but he still felt "insanely self-conscious" about his body.

Although everyone knew that he had artificial legs, he wore pants every day to cover them up. If someone made a passing comment about his legs, Liam says his heart rate would increase, his mind would fill with anxious thoughts, and he would try to withdraw from the conversation.

By high school, Liam was angry at the world because of how it treated him. He gave himself a licence to cause chaos. He had multiple car crashes, and was involved in selling weed at school. All the while, his mum, Trudi, was battling cancer – an illness that lasted for six years. Trudi died when Liam was 18, and his world collapsed. He partly blamed himself for his mum's death, because of all the stress he had caused her. But this was just the beginning of an intense period of grief. Within six months, Liam's uncle and great-aunt had died, and his dad lost his job. Having finished school, Liam was unemployed, on a benefit and consumed by depression and anxiety. On his worst days, he would only get out of bed for an hour or two.

"Questions were coming into my mind like, *What would it mean if I were to kill myself? What would the impact of that be? Is that something I should consider?* I felt like I had no hope. But in the back of my mind, I always believed that I

> could achieve something. So I reimagined myself. I literally sat down and brainstormed all the things I might be capable of doing – ridiculous ideas, from starting my own business to climbing Mount Cook."

Liam settled on the wildest option on his list: becoming a Paralympian. As a high-performance athlete, he would be able to build a new identity around the things his body *could* do, rather than simply being "disabled". To achieve this transformation, he set an impossible goal to reach the podium at the Rio de Janeiro Paralympics just three years later. On national TV, he promised to win a gold medal if the New Zealand public donated $30,000 to fund a set of custom-made blades. Kiwis from all over the country stumped up the cash, and Liam was ready to hit the track. But the hard work was up to him, and he knew he would be held accountable if he failed to deliver a result.

Liam had to swap his lifestyle – smoking weed, drinking a lot, eating bad food and staying up late – for the lifestyle of an elite athlete. It was a kind of experiment to see if he could turn his life around by designing a new character for himself. He spent weeks researching the habits, routines and behaviours of top athletes, and then he adopted their strategies in his own life. He started practising mindfulness to address the constant stream of self-destructive thoughts in his head. He regulated his sleep, nutrition and fitness. He learnt how to breathe and stretch to make his body more flexible. He surrounded himself with positive people who could mentor and encourage him. Eventually, Liam was ready to deal with his ultimate fear: wearing shorts in public and revealing his artificial legs.

> "It was horrifying. Before going to the track, I would curl up in a ball on my bed, and it would physically make me want to throw up. That's how anxious I was. But, when you practise mindfulness, you can observe those thoughts as they appear and as they disappear. It doesn't mean you can necessarily control the thoughts, but you can react better to them."

The road to Rio was excruciating. Liam didn't win any major races in the lead-up to the Paralympics. But when he got to Brazil, his discipline paid off. He won gold in the 200-metre and 400-metre events, and silver in the 100 metres, stunning the athletic community and earning him a spot in the history books. At just 22, Liam had beaten seasoned athletes who had been training all their lives, and he had broken two records set by the disgraced South African sprinter Oscar Pistorius. On the sidelines, Liam's charm and wit caught the attention of the world's media. (He described himself as "New Zealand's cyborg overlord" – one of the best phrases ever used in a trackside interview.) Becoming a blade-running machine had taken endurance, patience and grit – qualities that he never saw in himself before becoming an athlete. The discipline of professional sport allowed him to get on top of his feelings, rather than letting them control him.

A year after his glory in Rio, I interviewed Liam on Auckland's North Shore. We filmed him zipping around his regular track. He was still training hard, and sports pundits expected him to compete at the next Paralympics. But, just as quickly as his athletic career had begun, it was over. Liam shocked the world by retiring at the age of 24, having achieved the goals – and the personal transformation – he had set out to achieve. Since then, he has worked for an artificial-intelligence company, done an OE and begun a stand-up comedy career. He performed at the Edinburgh Festival Fringe, and wants to develop his performance skills even further. The man is in a constant state of reinvention. For those who believed his artificial legs would get in the way of a good life, it's clear that Liam has had the last laugh.

IDENTITY

*

When I came to accept that I had depression, I felt a sense of freedom. But as time went on, that word also became a burden. I thought I had depression in the same way that I had a backpack; every morning, I was obligated to pick up a sack of my emotions and carry it with me everywhere. As the weeks and months wore on, it became heavier and heavier. In the same way that a real backpack can pull on your spine and ruin your posture, my depression prevented me from standing up straight and moving around with ease. I thought there was no way to put it down – I just had to grit my teeth and endure its weight.

Because I was feeling sorry for myself, I chose to believe every negative thought that popped into my head. I allowed myself to sulk. I enjoyed feeling bitter, twisted and resentful. I was jealous of other people's happiness. I actively looked for opportunities to feel wounded. I made excuses for my lack of energy. And, despite the misery that came with all of this, I found a perverse kind of pleasure in wallowing in my pain. I became very attached to the idea that life sucked, and I sucked. I bought into the idea that I was broken beyond repair. I entertained these thoughts even though I knew they were damaging me, because they were seductive.

Although I never hurt myself physically, this amounted to a form of mental self-harm.

I became addicted to my own suffering. Some days, I would open the curtains in the morning and hope it was raining so I could add that to my list of grievances for the day. I would hope that my flight was cancelled so I could be upset at the inconvenience. Often, it took an hour for me to get dressed in the morning, and I would end up lying on the carpet. Fatigue is a common symptom of depression. But deep down, I knew that I was *allowing* myself to play the role of a depressed character. That was a self-fulfilling prophecy, because the more I behaved in a depressed way, the more depressed I felt. Eventually, being depressed felt more comfortable than being healthy.

It took a long time for me to realise that my feelings were manipulating me. Instead of giving in to them, I could do what Liam Malone did: choose to play a better character in my story. My true identity was much more than my depressive feelings, and that identity was still there – it was just buried beneath a mountain of pain. Despite experiencing mental distress, my values hadn't changed. Authenticity, creativity and connection were still really important to me, and I could return to those values. I could choose to see myself as a storyteller, a creator and a friend. I could choose to revive my sense of humour. And, as Liam did, I could even reinvent myself. My depression did not define me.

A character's identity is not their feelings.

9. CONNECTION

It was a searing summer afternoon in Los Angeles. High in the Hollywood Hills, the heat shimmered above the cobblestones lining the well-manicured lawns of the rich and famous. I knocked on the door of a glamorous mansion, tucked away in a quiet, leafy suburb. Inside, a local film crew was setting up cameras and lights. In the foyer, two actors were preparing for a scene. Tommy, aged 51, was taut and tanned. He strutted around in a white singlet, waiting for the cameras to roll. His co-star, 21-year-old Ana, was new to the industry. She was blonde, sweet and a little shy. The pair sat down on a bright red couch. The director called "Action!" Without missing a beat, they began to have sex – or at least something that looked like it.

I had travelled to California to report on the influence of the United States' lucrative porn industry. Adult entertainment is as old as the Hollywood Hills.

But, in the era of high-def video streaming, it has also become the main source of sex education for modern teens – and younger children. It's free, discreet and easy to access on any device with Wi-Fi. Health experts are worried about the impact of porn on developing minds and bodies. While adults understand that what they're watching is a performance, children and teens cannot make that distinction. Online porn is often aggressive, and watching it can shape unhealthy beliefs about consent and safety. Porn addiction has become a common condition among young men, and it can lead to erectile dysfunction.

None of this has deterred the porn studios. They are venturing into virtual reality so that home viewers wearing a headset can immerse themselves in live-action scenes. One of these studios allowed our crew to film the anatomy of a scene. Needless to say, it was the most uncomfortable assignment of my life. As the actors got down to business, my producer, Joanne, and I tucked ourselves behind a wall. Our cameraman, Joseph, stood in the doorway of the lounge, trying to film the performers in a way that was tasteful enough to meet New Zealand's broadcasting standards. Over a couple of hours, the actors had sex in a range of positions while the director barked instructions at them.

The process was distressing to watch. It was mechanical and passionless. No one seemed to be enjoying themselves – not even the male star. He told me that he had the most amazing job that any straight man could think of: getting paid to have "great sex with beautiful women in exotic locations". Tommy had been at the top of his game for 15 years, and he had a box full of awards to prove it. But, as we chatted by the pool in the mansion's backyard, I discovered the sad truths behind his lifestyle. Tommy relies on medication to "perform" throughout those long shoots. Working in the porn industry means he finds it difficult to hold down a relationship.

> "We're social creatures, right? Today, I came in and worked with a wonderful young lady. But I'll go home and shut the light out at night by myself. It's a lonely gig. It's hard for people to relate to me, because everyone thinks I've gotta be the happiest guy in the world, and that nothing can make me sad. But I'm missing someone to share my life with. I haven't made love in years."

Tommy and Ana both told me that porn sex wasn't "real sex". They had to follow the director's commands and pretend to enjoy themselves even if they were physically uncomfortable. For Ana, that skill didn't come easily. As the scene began, she struggled to know what to say or do. When she told the director that she felt nauseous, he coaxed her to keep going. After the filming was over, Ana told me that she moved to Los Angeles to get away from a toxic lifestyle in another state. As a fledgling porn star, she films three scenes a week. Ana said she sometimes feels "used" on set, but she feels "used in real life too". Being a porn star gave her a sense of power, but also made her feel more isolated.

> "For the first five months, I was pretty depressed. I couldn't have a real relationship – not just a sexual relationship, but friendships also. I just never thought that anyone could like me for me. I saw a doctor and he prescribed me a drug that helps with my mood swings and stuff, so I don't feel so alone and sad all the time."

Dusk was approaching as we packed up our gear and drove away from the mansion. It had been a sobering afternoon. We had watched an older man having sex with a young woman – a spectacle to be witnessed by tens of thousands of strangers, perhaps more. Both performers had told me that they enjoyed their jobs, but were also lonely. They seemed to be craving meaningful connection, and wanting people to recognise that their contribution to the world amounted to more than what they did with their bodies on camera. It struck me that porn does a bad job of meeting the emotional needs of its stars – as well as its audience – in a healthy way. On-screen sex is a poor substitute for genuine human connection.

*

Many of us rely on technology to make us feel closer to other people. There's something alluring about the warm glow of an iPhone screen, and the endless possibilities of being connected with friends, family, colleagues and strangers through social media and other platforms. Often, we're told that our society is more connected now than ever before. But I reckon we have been conned. Although we spend a lot of time online, that doesn't always translate to high-quality human interactions. Digital life can bring people together, but it can also trick us into believing that being Facebook friends with someone is the same thing as having a meaningful relationship with them.

Men can be particularly bad at keeping their friendships alive, especially with other men. In fact, many Kiwi guys don't think they need friends – they just need "mates"; guys they can do things with. Men are "doers" and women are "talkers", according to our cultural stereotypes. Male friendships are often built around rivalry, bravado, aggression, one-upmanship, beer and banter. Western culture has forced men to suppress their emotions. We can't articulate that we are desperate for nurturing. We can't admit that we have insecurities. We can't share our dreams for the future. If we do feel safe enough to be vulnerable, it's often within the context of a romantic relationship – away from other men.

It wasn't always like this in the West. In the 1700s and 1800s, it was common for men to share deep friendships that featured platonic expressions of love, like long hugs or even holding hands. They wrote tender letters expressing how much they valued each other. Back then, society understood that men's close friendships had a positive impact on their wellbeing, in the same way that women's friendships did. That began to change in the mid to late 1800s. Civil and cultural opposition to homosexuality caused men to fear any form of expression that could be interpreted in a sexual way. Their interactions became more distant and aloof. By the 1950s, society had become hostile to emotional intimacy between males, which was often interpreted as a statement about their sexuality.

Over the past three decades, the tide has gradually begun to turn. In the 1990s, we were introduced to the concept of a "bromance" – a term coined by the editor of a North American skateboarding magazine to describe the relationship between two guys who love spending quality time together. Hollywood produced a slew of buddy comedies. Popular culture gave us terms like "bro hug" and "man date". Those phrases hint at the idea that men desire deeper friendships, but the prefixes "bro" and "man" are used as caveats. In today's culture, male friendships are still usually depicted in a way that excludes vulnerability. We're reminded that men become connected with each other when they join a brotherhood: going to war, becoming part of a gang or playing in a rugby team. They're bound together by a shared intention to fight or beat something, not by their desire to meet each other's emotional needs.

In recent years, there has been a lot of media coverage about the prevalence of mental health issues like depression and anxiety among men. We know that New Zealand's suicide rate is disproportionately high for males. But we haven't joined the dots between these statistics and the social disconnection that many men experience. Loneliness is now considered a worldwide public health epidemic. It's linked to a range of poor mental and physical health outcomes for both males and females. And, just like smoking, loneliness is a killer – it puts you at a higher risk of an early death caused by a heart attack or a stroke. Despite these startling facts, loneliness remains an unspoken curse on the lives of many people.

*

As a young reporter, I was sent to a block of dilapidated council flats in Wellington to cover a grim story. Michael Clarke, an 86-year-old pensioner, had been found dead in his unit. He always chose to keep to himself, but his life had been so private that no one even noticed when he died. His body lay in his flat for over a year. It was only when council staff came knocking, to discuss a planned upgrade to the building, that they discovered the body, which had decomposed. The story was deeply upsetting, especially for the other residents in the complex. I interviewed some of them and discovered that their lives were also marked by social isolation.

Michael Clarke's funeral was attended by just 17 people, and only two of them had ever met the man. There were no stories about his life; no photos, anecdotes or mementos. Perhaps that's what he would have wanted. Perhaps being invisible to the community suited him just fine. But his death was a wake-up call for many Wellingtonians. We wondered: How could we have allowed someone to live out their final days with so little human contact? What did it say about *us* that we had allowed his body to remain in that unit for months? As a 21-year-old, I was disturbed by Michael's death, but I also knew that loneliness was common among the elderly. I didn't understand just how deeply it touched people of all ages and backgrounds.

A few weeks later, I was sitting in a taxi heading home from the airport after a stressful work trip. I asked the driver how his day had been. He launched into a story about his messy divorce and the custody battle over his two daughters, who he loved dearly. He felt that the system was pitted against him, and he was working long hours so he could pay his legal bills. I was exhausted and my brain was fried, but I knew this man's story was important to him. For 15 minutes, I tried to ask questions and engage with what he was telling me. But I was relieved when the taxi stopped outside my house. I took my suitcase out of the boot. "Hang on," the driver said. He pulled out a Whittaker's bag and placed two individually wrapped chocolates into the palm of my hand. "These are for people who listen," he said quietly.

*

Loneliness is not the absence of people. It's the sense of not being known or understood. Throughout my mental distress, I travelled a lot, and spent enough time around other people. But I felt separate. I didn't have the closeness or intimacy that I needed to feel safe. Even so, I struggled to accept that I was lonely. That word felt like an even greater taboo than depression. While I could blame my depression on a range of factors – including my brain chemistry – the word "loneliness" felt like a statement about my value as a human being. It was bound up with rejection and shame.

While I was depressed in Auckland, most of my close friends lived in other cities around the country. They knew that I was struggling, but I wanted to give them the opportunity to put a support system around me. In a late-night email to a very small group of mates, I spelt out, as explicitly as I could, what I was going through. I explained how they could work with each other to help me – by staying in contact with me, reminding me who I was, acknowledging my pain, and pointing me towards a hopeful future, even though I couldn't see one for myself. And I was brutally honest about the fact that my suicidal thoughts were intensifying.

> I have put so much energy into fighting to create the life I want. But, despite my best efforts, the growth in my personal life is at a standstill. Over the past fortnight, I've been fighting off the idea

that my death would be the only way to make the pain stop. This is a lie. But to me, this thought is like the light of a car's petrol tank when it is running on empty.

This group of friends promised to rally around me, and in the months that followed, they made an effort to do so. But their support was inconsistent, and I couldn't rely on it. I spent most weekends at home and sometimes heard from no one. Those guys failed to stay in regular contact with me, and they often admitted to being distracted by other things in their lives. I felt like I wasn't being heard. At times, I was tempted to physically hurt myself in order to get more attention. Those thoughts led me to believe that I was serious about dying.

I knew my mates loved me, and they wanted to help me get better. Some of them hadn't experienced mental distress, and couldn't relate to what I was going through. That's pretty common. Sometimes, people hold back because they're afraid of saying the wrong thing, or because they can't find a practical way to help. But what really hurt me was that, when everything became too hard, many of them became frustrated, so they just tapped out. They weren't willing to pull out all the stops to help me stay alive – and that was more painful than my depression itself. Their helplessness became my helplessness; it made me feel like my own efforts were futile. If the people closest to me had given up, then what reason did I have to keep fighting?

I already believed that I was a burden, and it seemed selfish to keep asking others to interrupt their own schedules to look after me. But it seemed I had no other option. I felt like I was drowning – silently screaming my lungs out while many of the people in my life stood in a line at the edge of the water, watching me sink. I felt like they were saying, "Good on you. You're doing really well. Just keep *not* drowning." I didn't have the energy to swim to safety, and I couldn't keep treading water. But it felt like I needed someone to pluck me out and drag me to safety. I thought I could only survive if there was some kind of intervention. When that didn't happen, I began to believe that my depression would ultimately claim my life – and it wouldn't be my fault.

*

There was one person who was willing to get in the water and swim alongside me: my best friend, Tommy Livingston. Many years earlier, Tommy and I had formed an unlikely friendship. He grew up in rural Waipukurau. I was a second-generation Kiwi from Lower Hutt. Despite coming from very different backgrounds, we found much in common. Neither of us fitted the stereotypes of ordinary Kiwi blokes. At high school, Tommy was mocked by his mates for swapping Saturday-morning rugby practice for piano lessons. We both wanted to build careers in journalism. We were creative and sensitive. We were kindred spirits, and throughout our twenties we shared all of the highs and lows that life presented.

When I became depressed, it was Tommy who showed up for me. Not because he was the "right" person to do so – in fact, there were others in my life who had more time, resources and life experience. The reason he showed up is simple: he chose to. Every day for weeks, then months, then years, Tommy was willing to be exposed to the raw, ugly nature of my distress. I was able to be honest, often in graphic terms, about what I was thinking and feeling. At times, we lived in the same city. Mostly, we didn't – but Tommy still stayed in touch with me every day, coaxing me to keep going. His words of encouragement, in text messages like this, gave me something to hold on to:

> It's going to be hard for a while. You will be okay, and I'm here for you. I'm encouraged that you hang on to hope. Your courage shines so clearly in your work. You remind your audience that

there is hope in the deepest despair – life to be lived, and love to be found. Thanks for being my role model and best mate. I believe in you more than you know.

In our stories, many of us are surrounded by people who are playing bit parts. Instead, we need strong supporting characters – people who are willing to play an active, consistent role in our stories. (We can play an important role in their stories too.) I knew that Tommy couldn't fix me. I just needed someone to recognise my pain, allow me to express it, and remind me that I wasn't going crazy. Having a sense of connection helped me to feel like I wasn't alone. On my worst days, Tommy's encouragement was just enough for me to get by.

Characters need each other.

10. SUFFERING

When Auckland Zoo invited me to do a story about two elderly lions, I leapt at the chance. Kura and Amira were mother and daughter, the last two members of a pride. The pair was inseparable, but that bond was about to be broken. Kura was old and frail, and the zoo's vets believed she was beginning to suffer. Over a period of weeks, our cameras followed the keepers as they made the difficult decision to euthanise their lion queen. But there was a catch: her daughter, Amira, couldn't be left alone because lions are social creatures. Nor could she be introduced to another pride, because she would likely be bullied or even killed. So, to prevent Amira's mental suffering after the death of her mother, the staff decided to euthanise both lions at the same time.

Two majestic lions. One in poor physical health, the other in good health. Both to be euthanised at dawn on a crisp Wednesday morning. I entered the silent, empty zoo, and watched the keepers preparing the injections that would put the lions to sleep. It was a tense moment. Many of the staff had spent years caring for these lions and were distraught at the prospect of ending the animals' lives. But they strongly believed that it was the best decision for the lions' welfare. Each lion was provided with her favourite meal, then two keepers entered the den and delivered the fatal injections. Outside the enclosure, the rest of the staff huddled, cried and consoled each other, until the lions' roars became quieter, and eventually ceased altogether.

A few minutes later, the keepers filed into the enclosure to say their goodbyes. Despite spending hours with these beautiful lions each day, they had never been in the same space as the animals because they would have been eaten alive. Now, the keepers were able to unlock the den and hug the lions while their large, furry bodies were still warm. Their first embraces were also their last. The lions' bodies were carried into a waiting ambulance and taken to the zoo's crematorium. It was one of the most emotional scenes I have witnessed – and the viewers at home were also moved by it. Many people told me that the story had touched them. They drew an obvious parallel between the lions' suffering and human suffering. If it's desirable for animals to be put out of their misery – including mental anguish – then don't humans deserve the same?

Suffering is a hallmark of human existence. Every generation in history has experienced it, and every major religion includes some form of teaching on it. For most of the world's population – including hundreds of millions of people in the developing world – suffering comes in the form of poverty, violence, war and oppression. These people don't have the luxury of making choices about where they live, how they spend their money or what kind of lifestyles they lead. They must fight for survival every single day, while learning to live *with* their suffering, rather than trying to alleviate or erase it.

In developed Western countries, however, we have a wider range of tools available. When difficult circumstances arise, many of us are privileged enough to be able to mitigate them. If you get hurt, you can take painkillers. If you get sick, there's free public healthcare. If you run out of money, you can take out a loan. If you lose your job, you can go on a benefit. If you're hungry, a food bank will help you out. Compared to the rest of the world, many of us live in a near-permanent state of comfort. We have bought into the idea that health and prosperity should be our default setting. In our stories, there's no room for suffering. In fact, I think most of us believe that we're entitled to live without it.

The reality is, however, no one can escape suffering. No matter how wealthy, smart or resourceful we are, most of us will face some form of serious pain or loss in our lifetimes. In developed countries, I reckon these events hit us so hard because we have been in denial. We have mistakenly believed that we're exempt from suffering. When bad things happen, we are emotionally unprepared to deal with them. We are devastated not just by suffering, but by the very *idea* of suffering. And, when those emotions feel unbearable, it can seem like the only option is to get away from it at any cost – even if that means death.

*

Throughout my depression, there were two questions that I was often asked: "Are you safe?" and "Do you need protection?" That's code for: "Are you about to kill yourself?" The person asking the question – a doctor, counsellor or friend – was trying to establish the possibility (or probability) that my death was imminent. Those questions were fair, but also incredibly naive. If someone is already thinking or talking about suicide, they cannot guarantee their own safety. Once you're in that zone, anything is possible. To a depressed person, suicidal thoughts can seem incredibly rational. If your greatest desire is to end your suffering, death can seem like a pretty effective way to achieve that.

But suffering looks very different when it is viewed through a storytelling lens. In the world of storytelling, suffering is vital to the development of a character. In fact, an author can only show us how strong a character really is by putting them *through* suffering. When placed in a perilous situation, a protagonist is forced to make decisions based on their values. They must draw on their reserves of strength and courage – qualities they may not typically display. Suffering forces them to take risks and develop endurance. After facing adversity, the character is more refined, and usually more confident in who they are and what they stand for.

When J. K. Rowling was asked what she would say to Harry Potter if she met him in real life, she replied, "I'd take him out for a meal and apologise for everything I put him through." Unlike J. K. Rowling, we do not get to control many of the events in our stories. But we do have control over how our characters respond to them. Like Harry, we are often overwhelmed by suffering. But, if we face it with courage, we discover that we're capable of enduring much more than we ever thought possible. That doesn't necessarily make hardship any easier to withstand, but it does mean that our stories can become richer and more meaningful through the difficulties we face.

Those lions at Auckland Zoo were wonderful creatures, but they weren't storytellers. Humans are, and that means we have an extraordinary advantage when it comes to dealing with adversity: we can use storytelling to keep us alive. To the teenage survivors of the Whakaari/White Island volcanic eruption, who are covered in burns and have lost their family members, we say, "Your story's not done yet." To survivors of sexual abuse, who live with trauma on a daily basis, we say, "Your story's not done yet." To those with physical disabilities that cause mental agony, we say, "Your story's not done yet." Even if you're exhausted. Even if you feel like there is nothing left to live for. If your heart still beats and your lungs still take in air, then you're alive – and we want you here. Your suffering cannot kill you – as long as you don't kill yourself.

*

There's a special bond between people who find themselves in a car together in the middle of the night. It was 2.45 am in Emerald, a small mining town in Queensland, Australia. I climbed into a rented Highlander with our producer, Steve, and cameraman, Martin. In the back, there was a small mountain of camera gear. For this trip, we had also packed steel-capped boots, fluoro vests and helmets. We had filled out a high-risk assessment, as ordered by our bosses. We had completed a rigorous safety course and learnt how to use our oxygen masks if something went wrong. This was no ordinary assignment. We were about to travel two kilometres underground, down a coalmine.

We reached Ensham Mine at 4 am. Already, a bunch of hard-looking men were piling their plates with enough food to sustain them through a gruelling 12-hour shift. As the sun began to creep up, we climbed into a "man-carrier" – a steel cage on wheels used to transport the workers underground. The cage rattled and groaned as it took us into the mouth of the mine. As we hurtled towards the blackness, Martin swung the camera towards the speck of light behind us. It faded into the distance, eventually dropping out of sight. Now, the only available light came from the torches on our helmets. I was reassured by the presence of one extra passenger in our vehicle, a person who had been on this frightening journey many times before. Daniel Rockhouse was an experienced Kiwi miner who had moved to Australia seven years earlier. He told me about his vivid memories from his first day at the mine.

"I was very, very anxious. Very nervous.

The noises, the smells, the feeling of going

underground – it made my heart pound through my chest. But one of the best things I ever did was to face that fear, and say, 'Screw you. You're not ruling my life.'"

Before relocating to Australia, Daniel worked on the West Coast of the South Island. His first mining job was at Pike River, a brand new mine built around a freshly discovered seam of coal that lay beneath a stunning national park. There, on the afternoon of 19 November 2010, Daniel was doing a regular shift underground, preparing to move a pile of gravel. It was a Friday, and his workmates were planning on hitting the pub after putting their tools down. The very next day, Daniel was going on holiday for a month, and he couldn't wait to have a breather – a break from all that heat and dust. But at 3.44 pm, everything changed. Pike River was rocked by an almighty blast.

"It was the loudest noise I'd ever heard, and it literally made me go deaf for some time afterwards. A shockwave hit me. It went through my body – it went through my bones. Within seconds, I was engulfed with thick white smoke. It was so putrid, so toxic. That's when I really started to panic."

Moments earlier, Daniel had been working alone in the mine's access tunnel. The blast knocked him out cold. When he came to his senses – up to 50 minutes after the explosion – he thought the engine of his loader had blown up. But Daniel soon realised that the blast had come from much deeper in the mine, where 29 other men were working. One of them was his 21-year-old brother, Ben Rockhouse. As Daniel struggled to breathe, he faced an impossible choice: walk further into the mine and try to save Ben and his mates, or walk towards the exit to save himself. Knowing he stood no chance if he tried to save his brother, Daniel headed for the exit. Along the way, he came across Russell Smith, another miner, who was nearly unconscious. Daniel practically carried Russell for one-and-a-half kilometres along the tunnel until they reached daylight. That short journey took around 46 minutes. At 5.26 pm, they walked out into the sunlight.

It was a feat that made world headlines. Daniel had survived a fatal explosion. What's more, he had saved another man's life, earning him the New Zealand Bravery Medal. This quiet, stoic country boy – just 24 years old at the time – had gained the status of a national hero. But in the process, he had lost his beloved brother and 28 of his mates. Daniel was diagnosed with post-traumatic stress disorder. His grief made him angry and dysfunctional, and it led to the collapse of his marriage. Consumed by what is known as survivor's guilt, he struggled to relate to his family and friends, who were also mourning their loved ones. Doctors prescribed a cocktail of antidepressants and anti-anxiety drugs to help him cope with his emotions. But even in his sleep, Daniel couldn't escape the nightmare he was living.

> "I'd have vivid dreams of trying to get to my brother. I would reach him, and I'd grab his hands. All of a sudden, the mine would blow up and I would see him get pulled into a fireball. Other dreams were about Russell. I was carrying him out, and we saw the light of the mine entrance. I would say, 'We're gonna make it!' Then the mine explodes again, and we're incinerated. Things got really dark for me. I was very much considering taking my own life. It seemed easier to end it. I'd just had enough."

Instead, Daniel made the brave and almost incomprehensible decision to return to underground mining. His family thought he was "crazy", but wanted Daniel to do whatever felt right to him. He strongly believed that part of his soul – his identity – was "still underground", and that he would only recover from the

Pike River Mine disaster by going back to the coalface. He moved to Queensland, and began working in mining communities where no one recognised him as the Pike River hero. Beneath the surface, where there were no TV cameras or prying eyes, Daniel was just one of the boys, covered in coal dust and willing to get his hands dirty – seven days a week, if necessary. As strange as it may seem, Daniel was back in his happy place.

At Ensham Mine, he showed me what a day of hard yakka really looks like. I struggled to keep up with Daniel as he moved with speed and ease through the wet, claustrophobic tunnels of the mine. It was clear that his workmates regarded him as a decent, kind, hard-working bloke. He earnt their respect, but it also seemed Daniel has learnt to respect himself. He fell in love with a Kiwi girl, Tammy, and got married. The horrific Pike River flashbacks still pop up from time to time, but he tells them to "piss off". In his spare time, Daniel does talks at other mines around Australia, using his story to encourage workers to follow good health-and-safety practices. None of this, of course, will bring his brother back. But the memory of Ben helps Daniel to keep moving.

> "Ben was a really good guy. He had the biggest heart that you'll ever see on a man. I wonder, *Why was it his time? Why wasn't it mine?*

I wonder what he did in his last moments. Did he suffer? Did he at least try to start walking out? Did somebody help him? Those questions are still with me. But I also don't want to miss out on the rest of my life. I want to make something of myself, and for my family to be proud of me. It's a slow road, but I'm getting there."

*

Hotel rooms are full of shadows. I've stayed in hundreds of them during my time as a reporter, and although life on the road sounds glamorous, it's usually the opposite – especially when you're depressed. At night, feeling weary and exhausted, I often found myself trapped inside a gilded cage stocked with KitKats. In the silence, it was easy for self-defeating thoughts to creep up on me. On a work trip to Wellington, that happened in a way I had never experienced before. I was staying at the Rydges Hotel. Room 1610 had a balcony with a stunning view of the CBD. From there, I could see the twinkling lights in the Beehive. I could see the TVNZ newsroom, where I began my career as a journalist – a place that was special to me. I could see many of the landmarks, restaurants and parks that I had fond memories of. The view was perfect. In fact, it seemed like the perfect place to end my life.

I wasn't surprised that I found myself standing on the balcony, with my hands gripping the railing. Depression had gnawed at me for more than three years. I had done plenty of stories about people who overcame their suicidal thoughts, and I used to believe that I could do the same. But I had also interviewed enough grieving family members to know that not everyone gets out of depression alive. Maybe I was one of those people. Maybe I just wasn't strong enough to survive. But the funny thing about suicide is you can always do it later. Perhaps depression is the only challenge in life that offers procrastinators an advantage.

I pulled myself away from the railing, and called Tommy, who was living in Wellington. He came to the hotel and closed the curtains so that I couldn't see the balcony, and he made two cups of tea. I knocked one of them over my bed. We sat in silence for a while. Over the previous year, we'd had regular conversations – often many times a day – about my suicidal thoughts. I knew that the amount of time and energy Tommy spent supporting me was taking a toll on him. But if our roles were reversed, I would have been fighting for his recovery too. When Tommy left the hotel later that night, he knew that I had calmed down enough to be safe by myself. Before going to bed, he sent me this text:

> Hey. I am really glad I was there for you tonight. I miss being able to be that person for you now we live in different cities. I meant what I said about you being brave. I hope you're able to have a solid sleep. Will call you tomorrow.

The next morning, I found myself hiding behind a pillar outside Te Papa museum, along with our cameraman, Andrew, waiting to surprise – and chase – the Minister of Immigration, who had been avoiding me. We were doing a story about the government's racist refugee policy, which discriminated against refugees from Africa and the Middle East. Five months later, that policy was scrapped, in part because of my reporting. I was only able to produce that story because I survived the previous night. I got out of bed, and I chose to play the character that I wanted to be.

I reckon we set ourselves up for failure by trying to live without suffering. Western medicine tends to operate on the presumption that things should be "fixed" or "cured". We expect someone to tell us that they can take all our pain away. In fact, we believe that life can only get "better" if our pain is completely gone. That's so unrealistic. Not all physical pain can be erased; sometimes, it can only be managed. It's the same for mental distress. Sometimes, we just have to find a way to live with it, while giving ourselves the best possible quality of life. We have the capacity to withstand huge amounts of pain – far more than we give ourselves credit for.

I had a breakthrough when I realised that I couldn't necessarily "cure" my depression – and that the pressure to do so was actually compounding my distress. All I could do was make choices that reaffirmed my true identity as the character I wanted to be, while seeking connection with other people. Those choices helped to make the really bad days a little easier. My pain didn't vanish, and I still felt exhausted, but I was a bit more confident about stepping out into the world each morning. I couldn't run, but I could walk with a limp – and that was better than staying in bed.

Suffering can't kill you.

11. MOTIVATION

Depression made me so obsessed with my brain that I almost forgot that my heart was broken. In my teens, I was diagnosed with supraventricular tachycardia, a condition that caused the electrical system in my heart to short-circuit. These episodes were often kick-started by stress or adrenaline. Just before I went on live TV or gave a speech, my heart would go into overdrive, reaching 250 beats per minute – triple the speed of my resting heart rate. I could feel my pulse throbbing in my ears, and I would start hyperventilating. There was only one way to make it stop: I had to lie on the floor, tense my muscles and hold my breath until I felt like I was about to pass out. After a few attempts, my heart would thud back into a normal rhythm. The condition wasn't life-threatening, but it sure got in the way.

A surgeon told me he could get rid of it. He would send a small wire up through my groin and into my heart. (Why does the groin always have to be involved?) If he could burn off the faulty electrical wiring, there was a good chance that my heart would stop bothering me. There were, of course, some risks. A one-in-200 chance that I would need a pacemaker for the rest of my life, a one-in-1000 chance of having a stroke and a one-in-1500 chance of dying. Death didn't bother me – after all, I was severely depressed. But the prospect of carking it on the operating table made me wonder if I should get my affairs in order. Did I need to update my will? Write goodbye letters? Claim the free coffee on my loyalty card? In the end, I didn't do any of those things. I just headed to the hospital.

A nurse shaved my chest, confiscated my phone and gave me a gown to wear. I was wheeled off to the theatre. Is there anything more disempowering than lying on your back and being pushed down a hospital corridor? Something was flashing before my eyes – maybe it was my life, or maybe it was just the fluorescent lights. Once I was on the table, seven people crowded around me. They covered me with wires and cables, then placed a mask over my face. As the anaesthetic trickled into my bloodstream, I was ready for some relief. Having spent months wrestling with suicidal thoughts, I was almost hopeful that I wouldn't wake up after the procedure.

Just a moment later, it seemed, I found myself alone in an empty ward. It was early evening, and I was groggy and confused. A nurse wandered in and told me that the surgery had been successful, but I had been under for five hours; much longer than expected. The surgeon had found two separate pieces of faulty circuitry. One was burnt off, and the other was frozen off. I had to stay in hospital overnight. I ate a cold sandwich and drank a cup of tea that the nurse gave me. The mug was inscribed with the words OVERWORKED AND UNDERPAID. I liked that she was using crockery to lament her employment conditions. I gazed out of the window at the Sky Tower. Dusk was approaching. I was still alive.

*

I've had some strange encounters with celebrities over the years, and interviewing Mel C from the Spice Girls is near the top of the list. She was performing in Hawke's Bay, more than a decade after "Spice fever" had swept the world. I decided to ask a risky opening question. I locked eyes with Sporty Spice and said, "Tell me what you want, what you really, really want." She stared at me blankly, and said, "World peace." I was incredulous at her cliché popstar response. "You asked me a bad question, so I gave you a stink answer," she shot back. I got what I deserved. But, although Mel C didn't like my question, it's an important one for everyone else. What do you really, really want?

I know what I *don't* want: the trappings of old age. Our society has pretty low ambitions for the elderly. In their so-called golden years, we expect old people to retire – not just from work, but also from living. Perhaps that's why many of them are expected to retreat to the safety of gated communities, where they can idly pass their time. According to our cultural stereotypes, old men are supposed to wear polo shirts and play golf. Old ladies must wear lavender and lace, and bake cheese scones. For many retirees, daily life revolves around naps, crosswords, *Coronation Street* and occasional outings to the supermarket.

Billie Jordan reckons these expectations are "repressive, prejudicial and ageist". In her early forties, she moved to Waiheke Island, just off the coast of Auckland, and discovered a community full of senior citizens who were bored, lonely and "behaving like invalids". She decided to set up a dance group to get them out of the house and connecting with each other. Billie drove around the island in her black van, rounding up anyone who looked 65 or older. They gathered in the local hall, expecting to learn how to do ballroom dancing. But these nanas and poppas were in for a shock.

Billie revealed that she wanted to create the world's oldest hip-hop crew – and she called it Hip Op-eration.

She dressed her new recruits in black T-shirts. (Some of the women in their seventies and eighties had never even worn a T-shirt before.) She hung silver chains around their necks and put caps on their heads – backwards, of course. With fluoro-coloured socks and basketball shoes, they were ready to hit the dance floor. Billie knew nothing about dancing, but she taught herself some hip-hop moves by watching YouTube clips and practising in front of her mirror. She choreographed a two-minute routine. Teens could have learnt it in a matter of hours, but it took Billie's elderly crew 12 months to master. In the routine, they had to scream and "bare their teeth like wild dogs". Billie wanted to present these old folk as staunch, powerful and "gangsta tough" – not frail, vulnerable and dependent.

> "I was acutely aware that some people would think it was cruel of me to put high expectations on the dancers. But why should your life come to an end when you become a senior citizen? Why should you shut yourself away in a village full of people who are waiting to die? I wanted to give them a sense of adventure. If they were twerking on stage and lost their false teeth, that was fine with me."

In the beginning, Billie's phone rang "from morning till night" with complaints from the dancers. They hated the music, the outfits and the moves. But she was running the class for free, and members could drop out at any time. Almost all of them were curious enough to keep showing up. After three months of rehearsals, they had discovered the excitement and camaraderie of being part of a dance crew. Media caught wind of the Hip Op-eration story, and TV cameras turned up at their rehearsals. Before long, the elderly dancers were taking their new careers very seriously. When one member had a stroke, he checked himself out of hospital the very next day, afraid that he would miss a rehearsal. When another member broke her pelvis, she was ready to bust her moves just six weeks later.

Before long, the crew received the invitation of a lifetime. The Taiwanese Government wanted all 22 dancers to perform at a major cultural festival in Taipei, in front of 14,000 people. I decided to tag along and film a story about this ambitious trip. Many of the dancers had never been overseas before. Some were deaf, some were blind and some had dementia. Between them, they had 17 fake hips and knees. But the prospect of illness – or even death – in a foreign country was no barrier. The group agreed that if a member had a heart attack and fell over in the middle of the performance the others would step over them and keep dancing. If any of them died in Taiwan, they would be cremated, and their ashes brought home in an ice-cream container. For Billie, who was the only supervisor on the trip, it was an anxious time, but she was determined to give the dancers a sense of freedom.

> "The Taiwanese hotel receptionist rang me at 3 am and said that one of my dancers, who was 95 years old, had just left the building. She said, 'Where is she going? What's she doing?' I said, 'Well, she's probably just going to the convenience store.' The receptionist goes, 'Aren't you going to do something?' I said, 'Well, if I do, then I've ruined the experience and killed the whole point of this trip.'"

Cameraman Byron and I stayed in the same hotel as the Hip Op-eration crew, and we filmed the dancers getting up to all kinds of mischief. They disrupted other guests in the lobby. They smuggled alcohol into their rooms. They learnt how to take selfies. They stuffed their faces with custard buns. They went to the local market and ate duck tongues. Without their family members or caregivers to fuss over them, they let loose – much to the surprise of their conservative Taiwanese hosts. It was like watching a bunch of schoolkids on a field trip. For the dancers who had experienced depression and disconnection in their old age, being part of the Hip Op-eration crew provided a major boost to their wellbeing. Billie reckons it even saved lives.

> "One of the women had been planning to kill herself. She had stockpiled her pills over a long period of time, and she felt there was nothing more to live for. But, after joining the crew, her life completely changed. Many months later, when we came back from an overseas trip, I said to her, 'So, do you still think about suicide?' She said, 'Don't be stupid. I haven't got *time* to kill myself.'"

*

The story of the Hip Op-eration crew was inspiring, but I discovered another powerful story behind it: the story of its founder. Billie had a tough childhood, and had survived sexual abuse. She experienced depression for much of her adult life, and by her thirties had become suicidal. After a counselling session one afternoon, she went home and wrote a suicide note addressed to her counsellor – the only person in the world she trusted.

Billie was full of self-hatred. She wasn't listed as an organ donor ("I didn't want anyone having the burden of taking my 38-year-old organs," she told me). Just as she was preparing to leave her house to go to the location where she would kill herself, Billie's phone rang.

> "It was my counsellor. Her instincts had told her that something was wrong. She sounded very urgent, and said, 'I'm coming round to your place.' I thought, 'Okay, she's already in the car, and if I kill myself now then she's going to be wasting petrol coming all the way over here. So I'll just get this over and done with, and then I'll kill myself after she leaves.'"

The two of them sat by the fire for hours, not saying much. Billie says it was the greatest act of kindness she had ever experienced. The counsellor had left her own family at night just to be with Billie in her distress and remind her that she was worth something. She says it undoubtedly saved her life. In the days that followed, the counsellor helped Billie to reconnect with her main values: kindness and compassion. Those values gave her something to live for. Six years later, she created Hip Op-eration because she wanted to make life less painful for other people. She wanted the dancers to experience connection and belonging – both of which were in short supply through much of her own life.

For many years, Billie took antidepressants. She says they reduced her pain, but also stopped her from experiencing joy. In recent months, she has weaned herself off the pills, and says she is the happiest she has been "in about a decade". Billie still sees a therapist every Friday, and occasionally has really bad days. But her character is no longer defined by mental distress. She sees herself as an advocate for the lost, lonely and disadvantaged; a woman who is able to use her own pain as a source of motivation for others. She was named Local Hero of the Year at the 2015 New Zealander of the Year Awards, and now spends all of her time speaking to business and community leaders about how to overcome adversity.

> "Sometimes when I was suicidal, it was my curiosity that stopped me from doing it. I thought, *What might happen if I don't kill myself? Would I win Lotto? Would I meet an amazing guy?* I just hung in there for a bit longer to see how things turned out. I thought, *If I get through the next five minutes, maybe the doorbell will ring and there'll be a crazy, wonderful thing on the other side of the door.*"

MOTIVATION

*

In our stories, some of us are playing boring characters who lack motivation. We want Xboxes and Lululemon pants and shower doors that are free of soap scum. Our desires don't extend very far, and our stories suffer as a result. Can you imagine watching a movie about a character whose biggest wish is to pay his mortgage? Or to save enough for her holiday? Or to survive another week in a retirement village? The arc of these stories would look like a flat line on a hospital monitor: stable and consistent, but lacking a pulse. When times get tough, our motivation needs to go even further than the desire to simply stay alive.

Every good character must want something. They must want it so badly that they will get out of bed each morning, no matter how broken they feel. They must want it enough to embark on a journey, quest or adventure. They must want it enough to risk their life, knowing they may fail. I have met plenty of characters like this, and almost all of them have one thing in common: they are motivated by something *bigger* than themselves. These people imagine how they can make the world a better place for others. Whether it's raising an awesome child, volunteering in the community, leading a great company or mentoring troubled kids, they are motivated by their desire to help others. It gives them fuel, even during periods of intense mental distress.

I have always been motivated to help people to make sense of their lives through storytelling. When I became depressed, I was tempted to cut back on my mental health journalism, because it often felt too close to home. But I kept producing those stories, because they gave me a sense of purpose. While I was depressed, I created TVNZ's first-ever mental health series, *The Inside Word*, a show that allowed ordinary Kiwis to talk about how they had responded to life's toughest challenges. I interviewed people who had been cyber-bullied, struggled with their body image, endured the stigma of teen parenthood, and escaped the grip of addiction.

The show had a tiny budget. I produced, presented and edited it in my spare time, and that process was pretty demanding. But I knew that I was creating something that could inspire people, and that brought me a bit of joy. Somehow, this little show found its way into the lives of people who really needed to see it. Viewers contacted me and explained how much the stories had encouraged them. A message from one woman stood out: "Over the last two weeks, my mental state has been on quite a decline. I was bordering on suicidal. And then I found *The Inside Word*, and watched it all on demand. It actually interrupted the downward spiral I was having."

That person – like the rest of the audience – had no idea that the host of the show was suicidal. But that wasn't relevant. Although I was struggling in my own life, I found enough motivation to make a contribution to the world. On a good day, I could even convince myself that the world needed me. I reckon the members of the Hip Op-eration crew discovered the same thing. When we spend too much time focusing on our own needs – especially on how they aren't being met – we feel empty. But when we're invested in the wellbeing of others, we always have unfinished business. And, as long as there is unfinished business, there's a reason to keep the story going.

Every character must want something great.

IV. Reshape your plot

12. CONFLICT

As my mental health deteriorated, there was one thing I hadn't tried: antidepressants. I hated the idea of taking pills, mainly because I'm a control freak. The prospect of putting chemicals into my brain, in order to change my mood, made me deeply uncomfortable. For months, I agonised over whether to give it a go. Eventually, when my distress became too much to handle, I asked my doctor to refer me to a psychiatrist. I turned up for my appointment at a plush clinic in a leafy suburb, where I would be charged $400 an hour. That seemed outrageous, but I didn't mind, because if I was going to try antidepressants, I wanted the very best advice. As I sat in the waiting room, I was unnerved by the song playing on the radio: The Verve's melancholy 1997 hit, "The Drugs Don't Work".

In the psychiatrist's office, I settled into a comfy leather chair and spent 45 minutes explaining my history and symptoms. He furiously took notes. At the end of my monologue, we agreed that it would be worth trying medication. But which drug to choose? I imagined there would only be a handful of possible options. To my surprise, the psychiatrist told me there were around 50 drugs he could give me, each targeting the brain's neurochemicals in different ways. All of the drugs were considered antidepressants, but he wasn't sure which one was the right fit for me. His job, he declared, was "more of an art than a science". I was gobsmacked. I hadn't asked him to produce a watercolour painting. I had asked him to tell me which powerful pharmaceutical product was suitable to put into my brain – my most precious organ.

He rattled off a list of drugs that are commonly used as first-line treatments for depression. The names sounded like magical incantations. (I could just imagine Hermione Granger pointing her wand at a mopey classmate and yelling, "Citalopram!" or "Fluoxetine!") I left the clinic with a prescription for the latter, which is commonly branded as Prozac and is one of the world's most-prescribed antidepressants. At a pharmacy down the road, the zany chemist made a real scene when she handed the box of pills to me in front of other customers. "Now, listen," she said, in a half-whisper, half-screech. "My husband swears by these. He says these pills should be gold-plated. If you feel a bit funny for the first few days, just persevere, okay? Things will come right. And remember, there is no stigma, you hear me? NO STIGMA!" I nodded, snatched the box from her and fled. Life, I hoped, was about to get better.

Prozac, a drug that has been on the market for three decades, is thought to work by regulating a mood chemical called serotonin. I took it religiously for a couple of months, but couldn't work out if it was making any difference. I went back to the psychiatrist and switched to another drug, Zyban, which targets a different chemical – dopamine. For a few weeks, it seemed to give me a bit more energy. Then came a warning bell. I began hearing a high-pitched ringing in my ears, especially when I was in a quiet room – the kind of noise that old people notice when their hearing starts failing. Tinnitus is one of the many listed side effects of Zyban. It was as if my body was gently saying, "This drug is not for you." I counted it as a blessing and, with the approval of the psychiatrist, I stopped taking the pills.

*

Every year, around one in nine New Zealand adults is prescribed antidepressants. A lucrative global industry has been built around the medicalisation of mental health and the widely accepted belief that depression is a clinical disorder associated with a chemical imbalance in the brain. And yet, when treating a depressed person, a doctor has no way of knowing *which* chemicals are out of whack. They prescribe drugs on the basis of their reported success rates – in the hope of hitting the right target. This process is hit-and-miss. However, for tens of thousands of people, antidepressants have made a huge difference. Many have told me that their medication balances them out, keeps them stable and allows them to function. For some, those pills have been a lifesaver.

But I also believe there are thousands of other people, including me, who have turned to these drugs in the mistaken belief that our brain chemistry is our main problem – or our only problem. Because of the widespread use and popularity of antidepressants, some people believe they need medication in order to recover from even mild distress over a short period. As one senior GP recently told me, "A patient will come to me and say, 'I want citalopram! My mum's on citalopram. My sister's on citalopram. Give me citalopram.' It's like saying, 'Here's ten dollars. Now give me my burger.'" Some of us fall into the trap of viewing our distress purely through a biomedical lens, believing that it has to do with our biology, and can be influenced by medicine. But we also need to use a psychosocial lens, which encompasses our emotions, environment and experience of the world.

There is no shame in taking an antidepressant. Chances are, you're on one right now. You may even credit that drug with saving your life – and if so, I believe you, and I celebrate the fact that you found it when you did. But I also believe that, while these drugs can relieve distress for some people, they cannot resolve the deeper issues in our lives. They cannot heal trauma. They cannot provide us with connection. They cannot help us to find meaning. By viewing depression solely as a chemical defect, we risk missing the underlying causes of our pain – and the chance of making a true recovery. Drugs can't fix a bad story.

*

TV reporters are used to being in hairy situations, but there's one assignment that everyone tries to get out of. It's called Helicopter Underwater Escape Training, a one-day course that teaches you how to survive a helicopter crash. The whole idea seemed daft to me. If I was in a chopper that slammed into the sea, I would only be capable of sending a tweet about it. But in the hope of learning how to save my own life, I went on the course. After a morning of theory, I put on a wetsuit and climbed into a large steel cage – simulating a helicopter – suspended above an indoor pool. The cage would be dropped into the water, before rolling left or right. Disoriented and unable to see properly, I was expected to undo my seatbelt, find the nearest door and swim to safety.

Really, there was no way to prepare for this. I took a gasp of air as the cage plunged into the water. I was trapped inside. Beneath the surface, I began to panic. I had rolled sideways – but which way? *Was the door above me or below me?* I fumbled with my seatbelt. As I tried to move away, something was holding me down. My wetsuit strap was snagged on the seat. I yanked it hard, then harder – but it wouldn't come free. I started to freak out. If the cord didn't release within seconds, I would pass out. Time slowed down, and everything around me became hazy. Just as I began to lose consciousness, an oxygen tube was violently shoved into my mouth, and I sucked in as much air as I could. I felt my wetsuit strap release me from my seat. A pair of hands pushed me out of the door and towards the pool's surface.

I felt pretty stupid. My safety hadn't been at risk, because there were divers in the water around me, and one inside the cage who was holding an oxygen tank in case I ran out of air. The instructor had warned us not to panic underwater. He explained that if we took a calm, slow, methodical approach, we would have no problem getting out of the "helicopter", even if something went wrong. I ignored that advice. My emotions got the better of me, and I lost my nerve. It's human nature to try to climb out of difficult situations as quickly as possible. But, by acting with haste, I put myself in a position in which I needed to be rescued. If I had chilled out and adjusted to my surroundings, the outcome could have been very different.

When mental distress showed up in my life, I looked for shortcuts that would allow me to get out of it as quickly as possible. Depression seemed like an interruption – an inconvenience – in my story. But, as I realised when I had a second attempt at the helicopter exercise, if you stay in the dark for a while, your eyes begin to adjust; you can see things more clearly, and you realise that you have the tools to survive. I think we're often in too much of a rush to move past our distress. We can lose some of the benefits, lessons and opportunities it presents to us. My depressed brain mustered up enough neurons to wonder: Was it possible that depression was making me into a stronger character? Was it possible that it was changing me for the better?

*

As winter approaches, Arthur's Pass becomes a place of wonder. The tiny township, tucked beneath the magnificent Southern Alps, is one of the country's most spectacular tourist destinations. Two months after the Christchurch terror attack, it hosted a very different crowd: a group of Muslim teenagers who had lost two of their friends in the massacre. It was the first time since the attack that the friends of 16-year-old Hamza Mustafa and 14-year-old Sayyad Milne had come together. On a three-day camp organised by Muslim leaders, the teens would have a chance to grieve, share stories and talk about the future. It was an intimate, private retreat, but the organisers invited me to film it. They wanted to show New Zealand that their community was beginning to heal.

Our cameraman, Andrew, and I arrived at the outdoor pursuits centre where the retreat was taking place. Bariz Shah, the 24-year-old president of the University of Canterbury Muslim Students' Association, was in charge. He told me that the young people were struggling to process what had happened. For many of them, reality had not yet sunk in, and the massacre seemed like a "surreal video game". As they huddled around the fireplace, some of the teens were laughing and joking. Others hid beneath their hoodies, silent and solemn. All of these boys had just been through an unprecedented traumatic event. Bariz wanted them to grieve for Hamza and Sayyad, but also to think constructively about their own futures.

> "I was in the burial team. I got to bury those boys with my own hands. Once the dirt went on top of them, it was like, 'Okay. Now the battle begins against all this negative energy that has been put on all of us. Are we just going to let this be bad? Or are we going to do something to change it?'"

Bariz is familiar with adversity. At the age of six, he moved to New Zealand from Afghanistan, when his family fled the civil conflict there. They settled in Auckland, where Bariz struggled to find his place in a new culture. He was bullied at school, but recalls having a "natural instinct to fight back". In the playground, he would never step away from a scrap, even if he was outnumbered. That fighting spirit is still an important part of his character. After the Christchurch terror attack, Bariz was determined to use the tragedy as a force for good. He was already mentoring dozens of Muslim boys in Christchurch, and he saw an opportunity to bring them together.

> "Our faith teaches us that there is no point dwelling on suffering if it makes us lose hope.

> **Suffering can change a person for the better, but it depends on how they reflect on it. Do they dwell on the negatives? Or do they try and find gems? I really believe that even when life throws awful things at us, our choices are powerful."**

In Arthur's Pass, the boys began to open up. They spoke – timidly, at first – about how tough the previous weeks had been, and how much they missed their deceased mates. Then, the tears began to flow. Over the course of three days, they ate beautiful hot meals, played games, went on hikes – and kept each other awake at night. When it was time to head back to Christchurch, they had made new friends and their faces looked a little brighter. In the following months, these young people continued to receive support from Bariz and other Muslim leaders. Many of the boys are now developing leadership skills in their schools and communities, and have expressed a desire to become leaders in this country.

The Christchurch terror attack didn't just transform the lives of those who were directly affected by it. It also changed the face of New Zealand. We began to explore and debate issues that had been swept under the rug for decades. We started talking about the prevalence of racism. About the failures of our intelligence services. About the threats posed by the alt-right. About the limits on hate speech. About the pitfalls of social media. It was as if Kiwis pulled together and said, "Let's allow this act of terror to transform us – and our country – in a positive way." Many of us let our prejudices be peeled away and, beneath those layers, we discovered compassion and kindness.

For Bariz, the Christchurch terror attack provided a reason to focus his energy on social change. He and his wife, Saba Afrasyabi, decided to create a project to honour the 51 people who lost their lives. They raised money from Kiwi donors and took it to Afghanistan, where they gave 51 people the resources to set up small businesses, such as manufacturing reusable bags or selling fruit in a custom-made cart. These people had been affected by poverty and war, and couldn't generate their own incomes. When they were selected for Bariz and Saba's initiative, they were overcome with gratitude – and even more astonished when they discovered that the project was part of the legacy of the terror attack. Bariz reckons this is exactly what the gunman would *not* have wanted.

> "I know it's a cliché, but life is a canvas. You are given certain colours, and you have no choice over which ones you've got. But you can mix those colours however you want. You can create

a picture that is to your liking. No one else can do that for you. You're the only one who has authority over your story."

*

We mistakenly believe that our stories are supposed to be free of conflict. But in fact, conflict is at the heart of every good story. It comes in so many different forms, including "human versus human", "human versus machine", "human versus nature" and "human versus self". When a character is forced to struggle, a chain of events is set in motion, and that's what advances the story's plot. A good story is not one in which bad things never happen. Rather, a good story involves a character who experiences conflict and allows it to transform them in a positive way. They grow and evolve. They are pushed, pulled and stretched in a thousand different ways. They are battered and bruised, but they are not broken. By the end of the story, they have become a stronger, more whole character.

Before depression, I was obsessed with my hectic lifestyle – knocking back coffee, flying around the country, yarning with strangers, being on TV and telling worthy stories. Hustling, flying and talking all the time. No one forced me to work that hard – not even my bosses. I enjoyed being busy because, in part, it fed my ego. I knew how to care for people, but I could also be cold, indifferent and overly blunt at times. I wasn't a bad person; I was just self-absorbed, like most of us are. But when I became depressed, I realised how complacent I had often been. Depression humbled me. It took away the emotional armour that I had hidden behind for years. The shallow, superficial aspects of my lifestyle quickly lost their appeal.

I came to an astonishing realisation: my distress was making me into a much better human. I discovered reserves of energy, wisdom and courage that I never knew I had. I became more sensitive to the needs of others, and could truly empathise with other people, because I had also felt deep pain. I started to see the good things in my life as gifts, rather than entitlements. And I began to experience the world in a richer way than ever before. I felt raw – as if my skin had been scoured away and my vital organs were exposed to the world. I was fragile, but I had been reduced to the core of myself. The essential parts of me – perhaps the best parts of me – remained.

Conflict can transform a character for the better.

13. MEANING

Katikati is a cute little town on the east coast of the North Island. It's famous for its colourful murals – 60 of them, all up – and avocado orchards – 500 in total. But, when I visited, another local feature was gaining attention: the Katikati Coffin Club. Every Wednesday morning, a group of old folk gathered in a large shed to share a pretty morbid task: building and decorating their own coffins. It was a thrifty hobby. Death can be bloody expensive, because funerals and burials are so costly. Having a DIY coffin makes that process more affordable. But the club's real purpose was to create a safe space for the elderly to have honest conversations about dying – a topic that is still taboo in many families.

I visited the Coffin Club while filming a documentary about ageing. When I arrived, I found dozens of people industriously working on their coffins – sawing, sanding and stapling with vigour. Each coffin was beautifully presented. Some were bright purple. Others were covered with pictures of trains or motorbikes. And amidst the dust and paint, there were hot cups of milky tea, sweet treats and plenty of black humour. ("We're makers of fine underground furniture," one of the organisers told me.) For each club member, the simple act of building a coffin was, in itself, an ode to living. It was a reminder that, even in the final season of life, there are still new people to meet, jobs to do and things to live for – even if one of those tasks is building a permanent home for your own corpse.

The concept of the Coffin Club was beautiful to me – and also comical. As someone who was severely depressed, it felt weird to be surrounded by people who were so chirpy when they talked about their own deaths. But, as I chatted with the club stalwarts, who had each paid a $10 "lifetime membership" fee, I discovered that some of them were struggling with their mental health. Surprisingly, they weren't afraid of dying; they were afraid of the prospect of having to keep living. One 87-year-old woman, who had recently had a stroke, told me that she had become "useless" to society. With no close family in New Zealand, she felt like her time was up.

> "I don't want to be here anymore. I would love to go now – before I get disabled and lonely. What's

> the point of me being here and soaking up all the money it costs to keep a person alive? I'm going to die anyway, so why not die now, instead of in three or four years, after a lot of suffering? I would love to have done to me what they do to sick dogs and cats – give me an injection so I go to sleep and don't wake up."

It was a startling admission. As the cameras rolled, I was caught off-guard, and my expression showed it. This lady spoke softly and gently, and her voice carried the pain of someone who felt lost – out of date, and out of touch. Someone who believed that the world would be a better place without them. Despite our very different lives – and almost 60 years between us – her story resonated deeply with me. I knew what it was like to feel worthless. Most of the time, I believed my own life was nearing an end. I had begun to think about possible methods to take my own life. Although I hadn't made a plan, I was getting fairly close to doing so. One of my texts to Tommy shows how unwell I had become:

> I just want to kill myself. I'm not going to be able to survive summer. I can't stay in Auckland, but I can't move back to Wellington. I can't keep working. I can't take drugs. I can't be alone. I can't

keep doing this. I don't want to be here any more.
I will never stop trying my best, but I don't know
how much longer I can last. The pain is unbearable.

*

In the early days of my depression, I tried to override my pain by seeking pleasure. I believed I could neutralise my negative emotions by doing things that made me feel good. I tried all the usual stuff: gorging on trashy food, drinking wine, watching tacky sitcoms and buying things that I didn't really need. Those pursuits offered me brief moments of relief, but they never lasted. I wondered: Was happiness really a prerequisite to my survival? Or was there another way to balance out my pain? Rather than chasing happiness, perhaps I could find meaning in my story, even if my distress continued.

Have you heard of "te whare tapa whā", the house with four walls? It's a Māori concept, developed by leading scholar Sir Mason Durie. The house is a model of human wholeness. Each of its four walls represents a key aspect of wellbeing: taha hinengaro (mental health), taha tinana (physical health), taha whānau (family health) and taha wairua (spiritual health). The latter encompasses all aspects of a person's inner world. For Māori, being connected to the environment is a really important part of spiritual wellbeing. Māori also treasure their culture, heritage and faith practices. In Māori culture, spiritual health is valued just as much as mental, physical and family health. The four walls reinforce each other. If one wall is weak, the house may collapse.

In secular Western culture, many of us have built our houses with only three walls. We are preoccupied with what may be wrong with our minds, bodies and relationships, but we are daunted by the prospect of exploring our spirituality. Perhaps that's because many people do not connect with the institutions and structures of organised religion. Nonetheless, we are all spiritual creatures. Each of us has some kind of framework that forms the basis of our relationship with the world and tells us how to exist within it. In the same way that we're responsible for our physical, mental and family health, we're also responsible for taking care of our spiritual health. But how do we do that?

There are plenty of ways to open yourself up to spirituality. Some people explore art, music or literature. Some people turn to history or science. Others participate in faith communities. In recent years, traditional spiritual practices and disciplines – including meditation, mindfulness, solitude and gratitude – have become popular in the West. It seems we are gradually becoming more comfortable with having conversations about spirituality in a non-threatening, non-judgemental way. Through spiritual practices, we can identify our beliefs and values. Our beliefs represent what is *true*, and our values represent what is *important*. If you have a clear idea of your beliefs and values, you can make decisions based on them – no matter what happens around you. Rather than solely pursuing material happiness, you can pursue meaning.

Most of the stories in this book are about people who returned to their beliefs and values when life became really tough. In doing so, they were able to make decisions that were meaningful to them. Bariz Shah set up a charitable project in his home country. Billie Jordan created the Hip Op-eration crew to combat loneliness. Karina Andrews decided to speak up for victims of sexual abuse. And the lady I met at the Katikati Coffin Club continued to build her own coffin, despite her distress. That decision – to show up, be with other people and commit to a project – reflected her values and affirmed her existence. It reminded me that I could still find meaning in my story, even if I couldn't be happy.

*

The heat was cruel. Dry, dense and unforgiving. I had just arrived in Colombo, the chaotic capital of Sri

Lanka. I would have been born in this city if a civil war hadn't forced my parents to move to New Zealand in the 1980s. Now, I was in Colombo as a journalist, trying to track down a reclusive Kiwi. Along with my producer, Jane, and cameraman, Cam, I made my way through the crowded streets. With beads of sweat dripping off our foreheads, we ducked between trucks and mopeds before arriving at a gate on a plain-looking street. Behind that gate, there was an orphanage – a sanctuary for vulnerable children run by Mother Teresa's order, the Missionaries of Charity. The nuns were dressed in pristine white saris. Among them was a sprightly older woman with pale skin and a cheeky smile. Her name was Sister Aroha. In Māori, aroha means love.

Before she was Sister Aroha, she was Philomene Hoban, a farm girl who grew up in North Canterbury as part of a close-knit Catholic family. Philomene was a schoolteacher, and brilliant at everything she turned her hand to, from cooking and entertaining to horse-riding and golf. She was charming, outspoken and a bit stroppy. Plenty of suitors tried to woo her. But in her twenties, Philomene decided to go travelling through Asia, where she was confronted by poverty. She recalls thinking, *Why are there so many people in the world who have nothing, while I have so much?* Back home, Philomene dropped a bombshell on her family: she was going to become a nun and work overseas. She joined the Missionaries of Charity, and served the poor in Australia, the Philippines and India, before being placed in Sri Lanka, where she has lived among the needy and sick for 30 years. At Prem Nivasa, the orphanage we visited, Sister Aroha was one of seven nuns looking after 60 children.

> "They've been abandoned in the hospital or on the road. Their mothers just cannot cope, and they have no means to support the child, so we bring them here. We can provide love and care for them. If you leave a child in bed, they will wilt like a flower and they may die. They need love. Without love, they will not survive."

Many of the children in the orphanage had complex needs. Some were recovering from severe trauma. Others had disabilities and medical conditions that meant they were close to death – or, as Sister Aroha put it, "in the waiting room for heaven". I watched as she stroked the foreheads of the children who were so unwell that they couldn't move or speak. "Was that a flicker of recognition in their eyes?" I asked. Could they tell that she was there, holding their hands? Sister Aroha smiled. She could not answer my questions, but she was determined to give each child the care and attention that they deserved, no matter how sick they were.

At the age of 75, most of us hope to be kicking back and enjoying our sunset years. But Sister Aroha worked 16 hours a day. Every morning, there were 60 sets of sheets to wash, and just as many hungry mouths to feed. There were no washing machines or dishwashers in the orphanage – everything was cleaned by hand. The nuns chose to stay poor in order to share the burdens of the people they served. They had no regular income, and relied solely on donations and goodwill – provenance, they said, that comes from God. And as for Sister Aroha's personal life? Well, she didn't have one. She had no access to TV, radio or newspapers. She shared a dorm with other nuns, and owned just three identical saris, a Bible and a prayer book. What she really treasured was her set of vows – commitments to poverty, chastity, obedience and wholehearted service. Those were her "possessions".

During Sister Aroha's time at the orphanage, around 2000 children had passed through its gates. Some were eventually returned to their birth parents. Others were adopted by families who could offer them stable futures. So many lives had been touched by this woman, a stranger who travelled from the bottom of the earth. Sister Aroha never rejected her Kiwi life. In fact, she spoke warmly about her upbringing, and the beauty of New Zealand's heartland. She dearly missed her family, especially her grandnieces and nephews.

Sister Aroha is only allowed to come home once every 10 years. Her next visit will be in 2024, but it's also possible that she will die in Sri Lanka without ever setting foot on home soil again. But she told me she had no regrets, and would continue to walk in the footsteps of Mother Teresa – the saint who taught her how to live well.

> "Mother Teresa was a really incredible person. She had so much influence on all of us. She would go up to people and take notice of even their smallest needs. I remember, in the Philippines once, a young girl was dying of tuberculosis. Mother said, 'Is there anything you want?' She said, 'Yeah, ice cream.' Before we knew it, there was enough ice cream for all the patients and many others as well. Mother always said, 'When someone is dying and they ask for something, give it to them.'"

On one level, Sister Aroha's life makes no sense. She gave up her comforts. She moved far away from her loved ones. And she took crazy risks – especially as a

Western woman – by travelling to dangerous places that were riddled with disease and conflict. Although this lifestyle may seem incomprehensible to many of us, it made perfect sense to Sister Aroha, because her decisions were based on her own spiritual framework. For her, faith wasn't just about blindly following a list of rules. Instead, it provided a roadmap – a way to understand her place in the world, and see where she was capable of going. By returning to her beliefs and values each day, she was able to find hope, even in dark places.

Despite working in such difficult conditions, this incredible woman had a lightness about her. She didn't seem to be carrying the world's problems on her shoulders. She knew what she was responsible for: putting rice into hungry mouths, placing shirts on the backs of homeless people, and wrapping her arms around children who needed protection. In doing so, she gained many of the things that the rest of us chase after: peace, contentment and fulfillment. I was struck by the contrast between Sister Aroha's life and my own. She was poor, but she was richer than I was. She was old, but her energy put my jetlag to shame. She was surrounded by poverty, but her smile was wider than mine. Her story wasn't grand, but it was filled with meaning.

*

Spirituality isn't limited to religious faith, but religious faith is one form of spirituality. I think Kiwis often look down on people who believe in a higher power, as if those people are looking for fairies at the bottom of their gardens, or running away from an old bearded man who wants to smite them with lightning bolts. In fact, billions of people around the world identify with some form of organised religion – and I'm one of them. I grew up in a Christian family, and my faith has always played a significant role in my life. Throughout my depression, I was able to remind myself that my life had value and that I was never alone.

You may be wondering, *Um, where was your God when you got depressed?* I think that question reflects our mistaken – but very human – desire to have all the answers about life. And my answer is: I can't explain my depression. I can't explain why bad things happen to good people. I can't explain the injustice that comes with suffering. But there is one thing I know for sure: I am in charge of my story. To me, God is not a puppeteer sitting on a cloud, pulling my strings. I have the intelligence and resourcefulness to make choices about how I respond to whatever life throws at me. I choose to believe that there is goodness in the world, that pain doesn't last forever, and that I am loved. My spirituality doesn't take away my pain, but it can help me to find meaning through that pain.

One wet, gloomy Sunday afternoon, I wandered down Ponsonby Road to Two Hands Tattoo, a popular tattoo studio. I showed the artist a very basic symbol of a cross. I laid down on the table and he started to etch the image onto the inside of my left wrist, using black ink. The lines of the cross were not solid; they were dotted, just like the markings on the side of a road. The image reminded me that, although there were gaps in my understanding of life, I could still see the outline – the shape – of what was important to me. Rather than focusing on what was missing from my story, I could focus on what was already there. Those are the bits that matter.

Beliefs and values determine meaning.

14. CONTAGION

When a disaster strikes, most people run away – but journalists run towards it. We arrive on the scene and hunt for people who may have a powerful story to tell. Usually, they're grieving. They're in shock. They're beginning to understand that their lives will never be the same. We must gain their trust, and make them feel safe enough to share their stories with the whole country. That's a tough task. The media is a highly competitive commercial industry, and reporters face pressure to secure "exclusive" stories – and get them on air ahead of other organisations. We have deadlines, and have to work fast in order to meet them. I have always tried to fulfil my professional obligations while upholding my own morals and ethics.

Yes, reporters do have ethics – contrary to what Donald Trump may tell you. Although we're often portrayed as vultures, most of us are good-hearted people with a strong sense of justice and a desire to give a voice to those who do not have one. However, our job requires us to meet people on the worst days of their lives. As a young reporter, I found myself in situations that I was not prepared for. When a group of students drowned on a school field trip, I sat in their high school's reception for two days until their mates who had survived were ready to be interviewed. When a teenage boy drank himself to death, I interviewed his siblings as they sat around the open casket in his bedroom, while rock music blasted from the stereo. And, when a young man lay in a coma in an intensive-care unit, his mother led me to his bedside. He never woke up.

For me, journalism is about searching for gold nuggets in the rubble of other people's lives. I am proud of my work over the past decade because, in each story, I have tried to give the audience a sense of hope. But many of my assignments have been overwhelmingly bleak. I have seen the devastating impacts of illness, crime, violence and misfortune, over and over again. When you spend a lot of time around tragedy, it sticks to you. It creeps under your skin and seeps into your bones. Although I thought I was unbreakable, I walked away from every interview carrying a fragment of that person's pain with me. After doing hundreds of stories, those pieces all added up.

*

A chocolate shop is an unlikely place for a terror attack. On a summer morning in 2014, a gunman entered the Lindt Café in Sydney and took ten customers and eight staff members hostage. Man Haron Monis was a religious fanatic who claimed he was acting on behalf of the Islamic State. Monis demanded to have a conversation with Australian Prime Minister Tony Abbott on live radio. Police wouldn't let that happen, and the siege continued. After six hours, the whole world was gripped by the chaos unfolding in Sydney. In the newsroom, my phone rang. It was my boss. He was sending me to Sydney on the next available flight. The problem was, there were no seats available that evening. I went home, packed a bag and spent an anxious night waiting for a red-eye flight the following morning.

When I arrived at Wellington Airport at 4 am, the siege was still underway in Sydney. By the time we got across the ditch, the story would still be unfolding. But moments later, a news alert popped up on my phone. It was all over. I panicked. A cameraman and I were about to get on an international flight. *What if no one has died in the siege? What if there is no story?* I kept hitting the refresh button on my phone until an alert came through to say the gunman had been killed, along with two hostages. When I boarded the plane, I was pumped full of adrenaline. That may sound strange, but these are the moments that journalists train for. In order for us to do our jobs, something bad usually has to happen first.

Just hours later, I was standing in front of the police cordon that stretched around the Lindt café. There were hundreds of bunches of flowers lining the street, and dozens of TV satellite trucks parked around the block. I filed a story, and did a live cross for *Seven Sharp*. When I came off-air, I collapsed into a taxi, satisfied that we had made our deadline, against the odds. But it also felt like a little part of me had died. I had learnt to do my job with a level of detachment, in order to protect myself. Just like other professionals who are exposed to trauma – such as nurses, firefighters and prison officers – I thrived in difficult, traumatic situations under pressure. But journalism was beginning to desensitise me to other people's suffering. What's more, it was starting to dehumanise me. At times, I *expected* bad things to happen. I could tell that the darkness in other people's stories was contaminating my own.

*

It took another six years – and the onset of depression – for me to reach a startling realisation: my mental health was being heavily influenced by the distressing stories that I was surrounded by. Journalism amplifies the awfulness in the world. (There's an old newsroom saying that "if it bleeds, it leads".) Not only was I reporting on people's deaths, but I was also reporting on people who were struggling to live. Having specialised in journalism about social issues – and, in particular, men's health – I interviewed plenty of Kiwis who had experienced crippling bouts of depression and anxiety. I listened as they explained the suffocating nature of their distress, and their deep sorrow about everything they had lost.

Of course, journalists aren't alone in being exposed to other people's distress. While it used to be taboo in our culture to openly discuss mental health, the pendulum has now swung the other way. These days, it seems like everyone is talking freely about their psychological wellbeing – on social media, around the water cooler, and at the dinner table. People casually drop vulnerable, confronting details into everyday conversations. They mention that they're in therapy, are taking antidepressants, or even that they have been experiencing suicidal thoughts. It's great that people feel comfortable enough to talk about their distress. That tells us that the stigma around mental health is beginning to lessen. However, as one doctor I spoke to recently asked, "We're letting it all hang out, but at what cost?"

Stories are contagious. They're easy to spread, and easy to catch. The language we use and the stories we tell can have a profound effect on the emotional lives of other people. For many years, I was surrounded by stories that highlighted the destructive nature of depression and suicidality, and those stories had a significant impact on my mental health. They contributed to my depressive outlook on the world and made my life even darker than it already was. The people I interviewed, the news reports I watched, the social media content I consumed, and the conversations I had with people who were struggling – much of it infected my own story with pessimism, apathy, helplessness and futility. There weren't enough good stories to balance out the bad ones.

*

I was on a work trip when I glanced at my phone and saw a text from a colleague in Auckland: *Have you heard about Greg Boyed?* Greg was one of TVNZ's most recognisable faces – a familiar presence in the living rooms of millions of people. I had worked with him for the first year of *Seven Sharp* – he was a host and I was a reporter. I was used to hearing Greg's voice in my earpiece when I did live crosses, and we exchanged traditional on-air banter. When my colleague texted me,

I had a sick feeling in my stomach. Before replying, I loaded up a news website. There, glowing on the home page, was Greg's face. He had taken his own life.

The country was in shock. Greg died while on holiday in Switzerland with his wife – a Swiss soul singer – and their three-year-old son. In a statement, his family said he had been "battling depression". Although Greg had left the airwaves, they were still humming with his presence. Workmates shared sweet, funny memories about the man they knew off-camera. Greg's closest friends described how he had confided in them, asked for help, and worked hard to improve his wellbeing. He tried to chase the light: running marathons, playing the drums and being a great dad.

For a man who had spent 25 years in front of a camera, it was a cruel irony that Greg's death became part of the insatiable news cycle. Journalists, paralysed by their own grief and confusion, did what seemed most obvious: they created more content. The internet was saturated with commentary and speculation about what may have led to his death. I found it all pretty overwhelming. I only knew Greg as a workmate, but I felt confronted by wall-to-wall media coverage of his death, as well as the grief of my colleagues. The pain of suicide was no longer "out there" somewhere – it was present in my workplace. Because I was struggling with my own suicidal thoughts, Greg's death was too close to home.

I had an email from a young woman who was triggered by the media coverage of Greg's suicide. She had been in a bad place for many weeks and was struggling to get through each day. Greg's death sent her "spinning". Even though she had never met him, this woman was deeply affected by the wave of social media posts, tributes, opinion pieces and images. She took sick leave and found herself at home on her own. Her trusted friends were all at work or out of town. Feeling "overwhelmed" and "completely alone", she sat in the dark for three days, holding an implement that she was tempted to use to kill herself. Eventually, she managed to stabilise her mental state – but she could easily have made the decision to end her life.

*

For decades, health researchers have argued about the existence of "suicide contagion", the idea that one person's suicide can lead to copycat suicides in their community. There's evidence that if young people are exposed to suicide – even by attending the funeral of a classmate or seeing social media posts about their death – they may be more inclined to take their own lives, especially if they are already in a vulnerable state. For many years, that evidence led the media to take a conservative approach to reporting on suicide. Journalists were encouraged to make the subject as invisible as possible.

In New Zealand, the tide began to turn in 2006, when former All Black Sir John Kirwan fronted a high-profile advertising campaign by sharing his own experience of depression and encouraging others to seek help. In 2009, comedian Mike King started a radio programme called *The Nutters Club*, in which he spoke candidly about his depression, and offered a platform for ordinary Kiwis to talk about their own experiences. Mike created the Key to Life Charitable Trust, and began speaking in high schools about mental health. Around the same time, the chief coroner, Neil MacLean, decided to release the national suicide statistics – an unprecedented decision that allowed public discussion about those figures for the very first time.

All of a sudden, the S-word, which had been swept under the carpet for generations, was out in the open. The media began investigating the country's shocking suicide statistics, and highlighted how stretched and under-resourced the mental health system was. We gave a voice to ordinary families who told powerful stories about how they had been affected by suicide. Today, there are still restrictions on how journalists can report on the circumstances of individual deaths, although health officials have loosened those rules in recent years. I am certain that these cultural changes have saved lives. As a journalist, it has been a privilege to contribute to the national conversation about mental health, and I believe our industry plays an important role in holding the government's decision-makers and health agencies to account.

However, through my own experience of depression, I have also realised that some of our efforts to bring suicide into the open have had unintended consequences. In particular, reporting on people who have died by suicide has the effect of drawing attention to suicide itself. By glorifying or oversimplifying the stories of people who have taken their own lives, we have often highlighted suicide in an unhelpful way. Media stories about the self-inflicted deaths of celebrities, such as chef Anthony Bourdain, Linkin Park frontman Chester Bennington or fashion designer Kate Spade, can be really triggering for people who have depression or other pre-existing risk factors. After Robin Williams's death in 2014, suicides in the United States spiked by 10 per cent over the following four months – a rise that researchers partly attributed to the extensive media coverage of the comedian's death. The rise was significant among men aged 30 to 44, and a disproportionate number used the same method of death that Williams reportedly used to take his life.

In popular culture, we are often exposed to unhelpful representations of suicide. Music superstar Billie Eilish, who is an icon for millions of teens, is just one of many artists who have been accused of romanticising suicidality, for example, in her song "Bury a Friend", which is about her own desire to end her life. Suicide is casually depicted in TV and movies – and even gets used in the titles of films that have nothing to do with it, like *Suicide Squad*. The language of suicide has entered our everyday vocabulary. At the height of my distress, someone said to me, "When I look at how thin you are, it makes me want to kill myself!" If you're in a stable mental state, these words don't matter. But if you're already looking for a way out, loose representations of suicide can easily become lodged in your mind.

We can't push suicide back under the rug. If we do, even more people will die, because they will be forced to suffer in silence. But there are hopeful and hopeless ways to talk about suicide. The stories that are the most useful for people are the ones that remind them that experiencing mental distress, and even having suicidal thoughts, doesn't make them crazy – and it's possible to survive. (Stories, I hope, like the ones that you have read in this book.) When we hear from people who have survived, we are reminded of our own strength. When we focus disproportionately on suicide itself, we reinforce a harmful narrative that depression always ends in death.

During the most intense period of my depression, I felt like I was the only passenger on an empty train. I hoped it would stop at the next station so that I could get off. But instead, the train passed through station after station, gathering speed. I came to the conclusion that I was stuck on board for the entire journey, and it was carrying me towards my own grave. I had written that futile, toxic narrative for myself, in part because of the depressing stories that I was surrounded by. But I had no idea that my story was also infecting someone else.

Stories are contagious.

15. ENDINGS

In many great stories, the supporting characters are overlooked – but they play a vital role in helping the main character to stay alive. My friend Tommy was alongside me for all four years of my mental distress. Even though we lived in different cities for most of that time, he stayed in contact with me every day. Some mornings, he would spend an hour on the phone to me before I even got out of bed. He listened as I described my unrelenting suicidal thoughts. And he spent hundreds of hours trying to find new ways to encourage and protect me. There were other friends who could have shared this role, and I asked them to do so. But those people did not – or could not – show up for me in the way that I needed them to, so Tommy stepped up to the mark.

He already had enough on his plate working as a crime reporter, covering gruelling court cases and breaking news. Tommy was also trying to build a life of his own. He got married, moved cities and began the process of working through his own challenges with the help of a counsellor. But, as a generous friend, he made sacrifices in his life in order to support me. Each day, he pushed aside his own feelings and needs in order to make time for me – and for other people in his life, who also relied on him for compassion and wisdom. His messages of encouragement, like this one, helped me to keep going:

> **There's no doubt you're in a far worse space than ever before. But there are other options than just killing yourself. I believe you can get through this. I know it doesn't feel like it. You're exhausted, and you feel like you're dying. But this is not how it ends.**

I knew that my distress was taking a toll on Tommy, and I tried to create healthier boundaries around our conversations. I hadn't stopped being *his* best friend, and I continued to be a supporting character in his story too. But there's no question that, for a couple of years, my distress became the focus of our friendship. I didn't understand how traumatic it was for Tommy to watch my life disintegrating. He knew that I could kill myself at any moment. Each night, he kept his phone under his pillow, just in case I called. I later learnt that he had already decided what he would say at my funeral.

On a winter afternoon in 2019, the frayed rubber band that held Tommy's life together snapped. At work, someone asked him, "How are you doing?" It's a simple, everyday question, but it was the first time in a long time that Tommy had considered it properly. He knew how everyone else was doing – but how was *he* doing? In that moment, his world crumbled. While sitting alone in a meeting room, he became overwhelmed with emotion. He felt like a failure. And a suicidal thought entered his head. Tommy knew it was just a thought, but it caught him by surprise. He went home, and in the following days' his life began to unravel. He became anxious, lost his appetite and couldn't concentrate or sleep. As he described it to me, a "thick, dark cloud descended very quickly".

I had often told Tommy that I felt like I was drowning. But I didn't realise that he was also struggling to swim. In hindsight, it was inevitable that my distress would affect him. It was never sustainable for one person to carry so much of my emotional baggage. I felt an incredible amount of guilt, because I had not been able to build a more effective support structure around myself. When you're experiencing mental distress, it's easy to lose perspective of how that distress is affecting the people who are close to you – especially if those people are trying their best to appear strong and stable. Tommy also understood that he had taken on more than he could handle; he had ignored the warning signs that his own mind was sending him because he didn't want to let me or anyone else in his life down.

Tommy had the support of his wife, Brooke. He took time off work. He went to the doctor. And he had more counselling – the very same things that he had helped me to do. I travelled to Wellington to spend some time with him. It was hard to see him so upset, but I was also confident that I could help him to recover.

I reminded him of the words that he had once shared with me: "This is not how it ends." As I said those words out loud, I was also speaking to myself.

Sometimes, it's not our own pain that brings us to our senses, but the pain experienced by the people we care about. Tommy's distress was like a shot in the arm for me. It snapped me out of my depressed stupor. *Is this really the kind of character I have become? Is this really the kind of story I have written for myself? Does it really have to be this bad?* I'd had a gutful of being depressed. I'd had a gutful of being suicidal. I was sick of my own story, and ashamed that I had allowed its plot to continue on such a bleak trajectory. I had to stop dithering and needed to make a decision: Was it time to end it?

Rob Mokaraka didn't want to kill himself. He wanted the police to do it for him. A messy breakup had pushed Rob into a spiral of "shame, guilt and failure", and he wanted the pain to stop. He says he had grown up "watching Māori men being shot by cops on the news", so he thought it would be easy to orchestrate the same fate. One morning, he dressed in camo pants and a trench coat, and wrapped a soup ladle in a tea towel. He wandered outside his house and called 111 on himself, claiming there was an armed offender on the loose. Within minutes, armed police – and TV cameras – surrounded Rob as he stood in the middle of the street. One of the police officers tried to build a rapport with him, by asking, "What's your name?" Rob was puzzled.

> "This officer was reaching out to me, trying to make a connection. He said, 'You're worth it.' I was like, 'Wow, this seems quite nice.' Then the old voice in my head said, 'He's a liar. He's full of shit. And you're full of shit, Rob. You deserve to die.' That was the narrative in my mind, and that's what I'd believed about myself for years. 'You're useless. You're shit.'"

Rob was used to being in the spotlight. He was a successful playwright and actor. As a performer, he learnt to use a mask to prevent people from seeing his true self. That mask stayed on, even around his friends and family. Behind it was a lifetime of pain, including childhood sexual abuse and "sporadic family violence, especially around alcohol". Rob had never spoken to anyone about these experiences. He had tried to take his own life on many occasions. By the time he called the police on himself at the age of 36, he was exhausted from covering up his emotions. With their guns pointed at him, the cops warned Rob not to take another step. He did – so they fired. A nine-millimetre bullet took him down.

> "I was lying in the middle of the road with a bullet in my chest. It was a searing, hot, burning pain that never stopped. It's like someone put an iron poker into a fire and then stabbed me with it. I thought, *I've made a terrible, terrible mistake.* The physical pain overrode the mental anguish, and now I had something else to worry about. My brain did not know how to comprehend the pain that my body was going through."

Rob woke up in hospital, where he began a long recovery. It took weeks for doctors to find the bullet, which was buried near his ribcage. As his body began to heal, Rob took the opportunity to unearth his mental trauma as well. He spoke to a therapist about events from his childhood that he had hidden for decades. It was a freeing experience, he says, especially as a Māori man who had been taught to shut down his emotions. Rob notes that in pre-European times, Māori had a strong storytelling culture. But colonisation forced Māori to suppress their stories and conform to dominant Pākehā narratives instead. He believes that this has contributed to the disproportionately high suicide rate for Māori. He almost became one of those statistics.

A decade on, Rob is a very different character. He's a man who "knows his life is worth something", despite his imperfections. He returned to the stage and transformed his mental health journey into a powerful one-man show called *Shot Bro: Confessions of a depressed bullet*, which chronicles his distress and how he overcame it. Rob has spent the past five years touring the country with this show. It has been a cathartic process for him, but even more transformative for the tens of thousands of people who have seen it – including me. Rob now helps community groups and businesses to have honest, safe conversations about mental wellbeing. He strongly believes that the power of storytelling can change lives – and save them.

"You need to get out whatever is stuck inside you. And you can do that by kōrero, by telling the story. The answers to your healing are actually in your trauma, and you need to explore it. It's okay to take medication, but that's like putting a Band-Aid over a bullet hole. And I know all about bullet holes. They just keep bleeding."

*

Sometimes, near the end of a movie, there's an unsettling moment when the music starts to change, the shots get longer, and you think, *Hang on. Surely this is not the end, is it? They had better not fade to black. This can't be the end.* There is no flashing light in the theatre that says: FINAL SCENE! You just know, deep in your gut, that it *feels* like an end – but the story is not done yet. If something's going to change, it needs to happen immediately. Someone needs to get rescued. Someone needs to fall in love. Someone needs to fire a gun, crack a code, break out of prison or catch a flight. Something important needs to happen for the story to be redeemed. In my own story, I was waiting for one of those breakthrough moments – but, after four years of unrelenting mental distress, it hadn't come.

On a Saturday evening in November 2019, it felt like the whole of Auckland was standing beneath the

Joshua Tree. U2 was in town, and there was nostalgia in the spring air. At Mt Smart Stadium, the four ageing rockers took to the stage in front of 30,000 people, including Prime Minister Jacinda Ardern. For the country and the world, another tumultuous year was drawing to a close, and it was time to celebrate. But my depression seemed to be reaching an almighty crescendo. As Bono belted out the aching lyrics of "I Still Haven't Found What I'm Looking For", I stood in the crowd, unable to stay present in my own body. It felt like I was watching the final scene of my own movie, with a rock legend performing the last song as the credits begin to roll.

The idea of suicide had always been comforting to me. It felt like there was a secret button that I could push at any time, like the button in Willy Wonka's glass elevator. I thought it could shoot me out of the roof and into the clouds. In a weird way, knowing that this button existed helped me to get through my worst days. And that's why, for so many months, my mind was filled with thoughts of ending my life. As those thoughts multiplied, they became more frequent and aggressive, crowding out the little space that was left in my brain. I was tired, anxious, jaded and overwhelmed. My tank was empty – mentally, physically, emotionally and spiritually. I had been strong for too long.

But there was a problem. If I ended my life, I would also end my story. My character would succumb to the dark forces that he had been fighting for four years. The tale would end abruptly. From a reader's perspective – and my own – my death would make for a deeply unsatisfying ending. As an author, I had spent so much time thinking about how my story would end that I had become distracted from my other responsibilities: creating a great character and writing a great plot. I knew that I could choose to focus on those things and release control of my ending. There were plenty of reasons to do so.

I hate pain. When it comes to physical distress of any sort, I have always been a total coward. The idea that I would voluntarily inflict any kind of pain on myself was crazy. I also knew the damage that my suicide would cause to others. Even though I felt disconnected from many of my friends, I knew that they genuinely cared about me and that their lives would be ripped apart by my death. They would blame themselves, and I would be responsible for the deterioration of their mental health – and perhaps even their deaths. Even though I felt like a burden and thought that other people would be better off without me, I knew that this wasn't true. I knew I would cause even more damage by taking my life – especially to my family, who loved me very much.

Most importantly, I believed in life. In my best frame of mind, there was no doubt that I would affirm life over death, and survival over surrender. I had spent years championing hope in other people's lives, and fighting against the evil forces that drag people into early graves. I had told hundreds of stories that reminded people that suffering is not fatal, and that even our worst experiences can be endured and sometimes overcome. To kill myself would be a total betrayal of my own beliefs and values. It would require me to abandon my quest to help other people to tell meaningful stories about their lives. I would never get the chance to find out whether a different ending could have been possible in my own story.

As darkness fell on Mt Smart Stadium, tears rolled down my cheeks. Bono leapt into a performance of "Beautiful Day" – clichéd, jarring but strangely soothing. It was blindingly obvious what I needed to do: I needed to take suicide off the table. There was no magic formula. All I had to do was make that choice, and let go of the ending of my story. From that point on, I committed myself to shutting down any thoughts that pointed to suicide as an option. It was okay to not get out of bed. It was okay to have meltdowns. It was okay to eat McDonald's. It was okay to be dysfunctional. It was okay to feel like a mess. But it was not okay to think about killing myself. That was the one thing that had to go. Rather than trying to survive so that I could tell a better story, I would tell a better story that could help me to survive.

Let go of the ending.

V. Release your ending

16. TRUST

It seems like a distant memory now – the All Blacks thrashing the Wallabies in the final of the 2015 Rugby World Cup. Rugby is a team sport, but if there was one man responsible for New Zealand's incredible 34–17 win, it was Dan Carter. He scored 19 points – through a drop goal, two conversions and four penalty shots – and earnt himself the title "man of the match". After the champagne had flowed and the ticker-tape parades were over, I sat down with Dan to interview him about his awesome performance. I wanted to know how he handled pressure on the field. After all, the stakes in a world cup final are ridiculously high. Glory is on the line, and a single player can be responsible for meeting (or crushing) the hopes of a nation.

Dan explained that the All Blacks had a not-so-secret weapon: Gilbert Enoka, the team's mental skills coach. Gilbert taught the players to block out any thoughts about the final score. Dwelling on the result would only lead to stress, anxiety, paralysis – and failure. Instead, he gave them a simple mantra: "Trust the process." The players were focused on following the systems they had developed during training. For Dan, that process became mechanical. Each time he attempted a kick, he broke that single task into a series of micro-steps, including his breathing, body position, eye movement and use of his muscles. His job was to execute each step in the correct order. If he focused on this process rather than on the outcome of the game, there was a good chance that the ball would sail over the posts.

Being the author of your own story involves trusting the storytelling process, even when it is difficult to do so. It's easy to be distracted by all the negative elements around us. Just as Dan had no control over his environment – the wind direction, the noise of the crowd or the quality of the ball – we have no control over the economy, the spread of illness or the attitudes of other people. But each day, we can choose to focus on what is within our control: building positive, hopeful narratives around the events that take place in our lives. When we trust that process, our stories take on lives of their own – and lead us to unexpected places.

*

The world is full of creative people who feel trapped in dead-end jobs. Jen Christiansen had a "soul-sucking corporate role" working in the call centre of a major telco. (Their phone number was "0800 ABUSE ME", she jokes.) To keep herself from going crazy, Jen picked up an unusual hobby: making delicate stone casts of children's hands and feet. She taught herself how to do it when her first son was born, because she wanted to preserve a physical memory of his little body. Before long, Jen's friends and family were asking her to make casts for their children. One day, she received a phone call from a local Waikato midwife, asking if she could provide a do-it-yourself kit.

> "I asked the midwife what it was for, and she said, 'Actually, it's for a stillborn child.' That hit me like a ton of bricks. I said, 'I would hate for you to use a do-it-yourself kit on a baby that has passed away, because it's not something you will get a second chance at.' I wanted to do it myself, to make sure it was done right."

When Jen arrived at the hospital, she was "terrified", and even wondered if anyone would notice if she ran away. She was about to walk into a deeply private moment of grief. She wasn't sure how the family would feel about her presence. Even though the little boy had passed away, Jen knew that his parents would be protective of him. She needed them to trust her to hold and care for their precious son in a respectful way. As she approached the ward, Jen's heart was racing and her arms were shaking. She tried to calm those nerves and make herself look professional, before taking a deep breath and walking into the room.

> "Instead of finding the intense sadness that I had expected, I found love and joy. Although their child had passed, they were still welcoming him as part of the family. It was a peaceful experience. The child was not crying, and he wasn't in pain. The mum left the room and allowed me to do my job. On the way home, I was crying and smiling. I felt so much sadness for the family, but a lot of joy for what I was able to give them."

Jen created a charity, Angel Casts, which provides a free service for bereaved parents. She makes casts of their child's hands and feet, at no cost. Over the past five years, she has received phone calls at all hours of the day and night from midwives across the Waikato. If a baby dies at 3 am and is being sent for a post-mortem at 5 am, Jen will climb out of bed and sneak out of the house, leaving behind her husband, Aaron, and their five kids. Often, she will be back in bed by 6 am, and they won't even know that she was gone. Jen has to get her kids ready for school, "while pretending that mummy has had a full night's sleep". At her busiest, she's called to the hospital up to three times a day.

Angel Casts relies solely on donations. For the first few years of the charity, Jen didn't take a wage from it, because there was no form of regular income. In fact, she and Aaron used up their own savings to keep the service running and have dedicated thousands of hours of free labour to it. This took a huge toll on their family, but they knew they could help so many other families that had been affected by grief. All up, Jen has cast the hands and feet of more than 550 dead children. She tries not to keep count, because that number is overwhelming. Most of the children were stillborn, but she also sees older kids, including those who have died from cancer or an accident.

This is not the lifestyle that Jen had planned, and it often feels crushing. Some days, she finds it difficult to even answer her phone; she just cannot face the prospect of meeting another family that has been devastated by loss. But she always finds the strength to return the call, because she hates the idea of any family missing out on the chance to preserve their child's memory. Each time she drives to the hospital, Jen tries to leave her own emotions "in the car", because, when she meets a new family, she wants to be fresh, alert and ready to offer compassion and attention.

As a mum of five, Jen's work has given her a new appreciation for the gift of parenthood. Sometimes, it also makes her overprotective. If she sees one of her kids playing in the front seat of the car, it terrifies her, because she has seen a dead child who released a handbrake and was run over when he tried to escape the moving vehicle. When her baby is in the bath, she makes sure her hands are on the baby at all times, because she has seen dead children who drowned in the bath. Jen knows that she can't allow her life to be ruled by fear. Before her kids go to bed, she spends as much time with them as possible, singing an extra song or reading an extra book. She reminds herself that life can be good, even for those who have suffered immense loss.

Jen has experienced her own grief. Her brother Andrew died at the age of 27, after a long battle with depression. The pair had a close relationship, and Andrew had a great sense of humour. But Jen says her brother struggled with his sense of self-worth, and that he "didn't expose himself to real relationships, and wasn't looking after his body". She supported him through many years of mental distress, and helped him to survive after multiple suicide attempts. Late at night, they had long conversations in which Andrew shared that he felt like a burden. When he died, Jen was hit by a wave of grief, but she recognised that she could choose how to respond to Andrew's death. By making casts, she is able to remind other people that losing a loved one doesn't mean that your own life has to be over.

> "There's always a glimmer of light in really dark times, and it brings people closer together. I've created friendships with people I've met on the worst days of their lives. For those families, there can still be hope, there can be joy, there can be so much to look forward to. No matter what happens in life, you can't just dig your heels in the sand and say, 'This is the end of me.' There is always more life to be had."

*

There's a curious phenomenon in the animal kingdom, where creatures that have been locked in cages for a long time can become psychologically trapped in those environments. If a bird has spent its life behind bars, it may become "cage-bound". Even if the door is left wide open, the bird will not realise that it can escape – or it may not have the courage to do so. These animals have been damaged by their isolation. They often become aggressive and self-destructive, plucking their own feathers and even self-mutilating. A cage-bound bird is paralysed by its fear of the outside world and prefers the relative safety of the cage, even if that environment is harmful.

Depression tricked me into feeling safe in my own cage. I felt imprisoned in my unhealthy lifestyle, but I accepted the confines of my existence. I clung to everything that felt comfortable and familiar. I stayed in my job, even though it had stopped bringing me joy. I stayed in my flat, even though I spent most of my time in bed. And I stayed in Auckland, even though I was far from my friends and family. I felt trapped and helpless. But really, no one was forcing me to live like this. I had chosen to stay in an environment that continued to bring me suffering, and I hadn't taken responsibility for that choice.

For months, I agonised over whether I could leave. Could I give up my busy lifestyle? Could I give up my job, and the sense of purpose and influence it gave me? I didn't think so. My work was the only thing that was holding my life together. I relied on it to give me a reason to get out of bed each morning. But by October 2019, I was completely spent, and I knew I couldn't keep going. I met with my bosses at TVNZ and told them that I needed some time off. Not just a holiday. I asked for six months off – the longest break since I started working during my teens. I didn't have the courage to tell them that I was suicidal. Instead, I said I was tired, exhausted, drained, fried, burnt-out. They were good enough to give me six months of unpaid leave.

My so-called break piqued my colleagues' curiosity. Most of them were unaware of my mental health struggles, and couldn't understand what I was up to. Why was I taking time off? Where was I going? What was I going to do for six months? What would happen to my career? I fended off those questions, mainly because I didn't have the answers. I just needed to get out. Out of my job, out of the city, out of the lifestyle that was killing me. I cleaned out my desk and left the Auckland newsroom, carrying a bag of notebooks and awards, and my gumboots (during a decade on TV, I had worn them twice). I was sad and confused, but hoped that I would be back six months later – healthier, happier and ready to have another crack at my old life.

*

On a Thursday morning in December 2019, I woke up at 4.30 am. I packed my car with clothes and furniture –

the same stuff I had brought to Auckland four years earlier. I drove to Wellington, where I would spend my six-month break. I planned to disappear from sight. I would stop working, and instead, I would just try to recover. Making the decision to move home was the toughest call of my life. At 26, I had left that city as an energetic, ambitious young journalist chasing a bright future in Auckland. I was returning at the age of 30, broken, exhausted and defeated.

I rented a small studio apartment in the city. For six months, I had nothing to do, and all the time in the world to do it. I knew that I needed to design a new daily routine – one that was robust enough to give me a sense of purpose. Each morning, I forced myself to leave the apartment. I took myself out for coffee. I built my fitness back up to five-kilometre runs. I cooked proper meals for the first time in years. Most days, I didn't feel like doing any of this. But I kept asking myself, "What would a good character do?" I tried to write a hopeful story – and then live *into* that story. On any given day, if my biggest achievement was going for a 15-minute walk, I could still tell a better story at the end of that day than if I had stayed in bed.

My working life has always revolved around noise, activity and constant stimulation. But when I moved back to Wellington, I began to adapt to a whole new way of living. I could spend long periods sitting in silence. I could even spend a whole day without talking to anyone – and, to my surprise, I was okay with it. As summer rolled on, I spent hundreds of hours staring out of the window of my apartment. From the 18th floor, there was a vast, unobstructed view of the city. In the evenings, the sunset would descend on the hills like a warm blanket. Some days, this stunning view was deeply moving. On other days, the apartment window felt like an exit route, and I would have to pull myself away. I told myself that I was safe in my own company.

Without the pressure of my job, I felt adrift. I often wondered if I had made a terrible mistake. I contemplated putting the pieces of my old life back together by returning to Auckland, returning to TV – and, I guess, returning to the worst stage of my depression. (It almost seemed better to have a dysfunctional life than no life at all.) But I knew that I couldn't go back straight away. I had to find a way to survive this new chapter, and trust that my daily habits and routines – as boring as they seemed – were leading me back to health. My story was beginning to change, and I could also feel something changing within me.

Trust the process.

17. ACCEPTANCE

Some years ago, I was arguing with a colleague about a story we were working on. He leant back in his chair and sighed, "Why do *all* of your stories need a redemptive arc?" It was meant as a criticism, but I took it as a compliment. He was right: my stories focused on redemption. Each character found a way to overcome their pain. They chose to focus on the positive things in their lives. They became stronger as a result of their suffering. The reason I tell redemptive stories is that they reflect my own worldview. I believe that life *can* get better, and that good things can come from terrible experiences. How bleak the world would be if we didn't believe that redemption was possible.

In the media, most "human interest" stories have the same arc: Someone falls in a hole, then climbs out of it. They survive. They recover. Their problems are gone, or at least significantly diminished. Real life rarely unfolds in such a clean way, but journalists often oversimplify events because we need to reduce them to a neat little TV-friendly package. We want to present the audience with a story that has a resolution and, ideally, a happy ending. Maybe that's what my colleague meant. We can't always find a happy ending in our stories. Some people who get cancer will never recover. Some people who are injured will never walk again. Some people who try to have children will never be able to.

It can be difficult to find positive meaning – or any meaning – in these kinds of events. But a story can still be meaningful even if it doesn't have a satisfying resolution. When life stays the same – or even gets worse – we can choose to accept the cards that we have been dealt, and play them in the smartest, most creative way possible. We can always redeem our stories – not necessarily by triumphing over adversity, but by coming to terms with what we have lost, and choosing to keep going.

*

If you were carrying a killer gene, would you want to know? Or would you prefer to live in blissful ignorance? When I met 29-year-old Micheal Hanly, he was wrestling with this dilemma. Micheal's father had just been diagnosed with Huntington's disease, a condition that causes a person to gradually lose control of their body and mind. The disease has no cure, and usually a patient will only live for about 20 years after their symptoms begin. For Micheal, this was devastating news. His father's body was already beginning to deteriorate. But Micheal was also grappling with another startling fact: there was a 50 per cent chance that he had inherited the disease from his dad, meaning he also faced the prospect of a slow, painful early death.

I asked Micheal to be interviewed for a story about the impact of Huntington's disease on Kiwi families. When we met, he was a wreck. He had just broken up with his girlfriend and sold the house – and the cat – they shared. He was living at home with his parents, who were struggling emotionally. The family home was spacious and beautiful, but it ached with grief. Micheal agonised over whether to get tested. Eventually, he chose to do it, in the hope of having some certainty about what his future would look like. He was nervous about the result, but he knew it would allow him to make plans for the years ahead.

When the day of reckoning arrived, Micheal woke up at 4 am. Full of nerves, he decided to run up Mount Eden, in the Auckland neighbourhood he grew up in. He reached the top of the mountain just before dawn. There, while breathing heavily and crying, he watched the sun come up, and reflected on his life – a moment that was both "oddly romantic" and "super emotional". After his run, Micheal prepared for his 10 am appointment at Auckland Hospital. On the way there, his heart raced and he was sweating profusely. At the hospital, he couldn't find a park. ("I was nearly late to find out if I had a terminal illness," he joked.) Inside, a counsellor sat down with Micheal to present him with the results of his test. A sealed envelope contained his fate.

> "She opened the envelope and said, 'I'm very sorry. You tested positive.' It was like being struck by lightning. It was so shocking that I was crying before I even realised what had happened. It was complete and utter anguish, devastation and horror. I couldn't believe it."

The rest of the week was a blur. Micheal contacted his boss and took two weeks off work to recover from the shock of his diagnosis. Nothing felt real. Even normal activities, like watching TV or going for a walk, felt meaningless. He says he didn't consider suicide, but at his lowest point thought, *I don't know why I'm here anymore. I feel like there is nothing left.* Micheal had always dreamt of becoming a father, but now he had a 50 per cent chance of passing his condition on to any future children. He couldn't imagine having a child under those circumstances. In fact, he couldn't even imagine that any woman would be able to love him. Every time he thought about going on a date, he felt worthless.

> "I was like, 'I don't stand a chance.' I've been diagnosed with an illness that might mean I die at a very young age, or simply lose my capacity to live, and I will no longer be the person she fell in love with. What's the point in going on a first date if on the second or third date you have to tell her this? The fear of rejection was intense. I didn't feel there was much hope for me."

Two years after his diagnosis, one of Micheal's friends introduced him to a woman named Pia, a Kiwi diplomat who was about to move to Mexico for a job in the New Zealand embassy. They hit it off, and he decided to follow her to Mexico. For the past year, they have lived together in Polanco, the "Beverly Hills of Mexico", where Micheal works from home as a freelance designer. His worries have melted away, and, for the first time in years, he feels confident enough to be himself. He exercises. He meditates. He cooks.

He's learning Spanish. And he uses his Huntington's diagnosis as motivation to do the things on his bucket list, from skydiving to scuba-diving. Micheal wants to take good care of his body and mind. For now, he has no Huntington's symptoms. His dad's condition showed up in his late fifties, so Micheal hopes he will be symptom-free for another couple of decades.

He will soon have another reason to stay active: he's about to become a father. Pia's pregnancy was a surprise. She has polycystic ovarian syndrome and was told by doctors that her chance of conceiving a child was extremely slim. Against the odds, she fell pregnant. Because of Micheal's condition, doctors offered to screen the foetus for the Huntington's gene, allowing the couple to terminate the pregnancy if the test was positive. They refused the test. Rather than contemplating whether his baby will have Huntington's, Micheal is thinking about what kind of dad he wants to be. He's looking forward to doing the same things that his father once did with him – taking his child to beautiful beaches, teaching them how to play, and trying to make them laugh.

> "There is so much joy around the pregnancy. Not just for us, but for my parents. It's the first time something really good has happened to them for years. I hope I will be a good dad. And I hope

that once my child grows up, if they do have the Huntington's gene, there will be medication to allow them to live a normal life. There will be lots of hurdles to overcome, but I'm not worried. It's going to be a great big uncertain adventure."

Micheal's story turned out pretty well, in the sense that he got what he wanted: a partner, a baby and a sweet life in Mexico. But I think this interpretation cheapens the value of his story. The moral of the story is not that Micheal got what he wanted, it's that he chose to keep living, even *before* there were any signs of positive change. Faced with a terminal diagnosis, many of us would have thrown our hands in the air and said, "Oh well, I'm probably going to die early. What could possibly be worth getting out of bed for?" Instead, Micheal accepted his diagnosis, and kept making choices that affirmed the value of his life. He made his story matter.

We often describe our challenges in such a black-and-white way. We talk about people "beating" cancer or "fighting" depression. This kind of language implies that there are always winners and losers: those who come out on top, and those who are defeated. But most of us are forced to live in life's grey areas. Micheal has Huntington's disease, and there is no way to "beat" or "fight" it. In some ways, a happy ending is impossible, because there is no cure. But even though his story doesn't offer a triumphant moment of victory, it demonstrates the power of acceptance. Is there anything more courageous than accepting a fate that involves suffering? Is there anything more heroic than choosing to keep living in the face of death?

*

Edgecumbe is a small town in the Bay of Plenty. On a Thursday morning in April 2017, a swollen river put pressure on a concrete stopbank, which first cracked, then snapped, sending a torrent of water into the township. The residents had just minutes to grab a few belongings and their pets before fleeing by car or on foot. A few days later, as the water began to recede, I travelled to Edgecumbe to report on the recovery. A rotten stench hung in the air, and the streets were covered with debris from the two-metre-high flood. The water had emptied many homes of their contents. Furniture, toys, paperwork and mementos were strewn everywhere.

I watched the locals returning to their damaged homes. They stood on their front lawns in silence, staring at the mess that lay in front of them. Many families' furniture and belongings were contaminated with raw sewage and had to be thrown out. Some of the houses had to be demolished. Many locals had to accept that they would never be able to put their homes back to the way they had been before the flood. They had to come to terms with what they had lost. Then – and only then – could they imagine what the future looked like.

In my own life, depression was a flood that seeped into every corner of my being and dragged away many of the things that were precious to me. I wasted a lot of time trying to put everything back in the right place. But, when I returned to Wellington, I had to accept that I wouldn't necessarily be able to achieve that. In my apartment, I often felt like I was trapped in a prison cell or a hospital ward. I knew it was possible that I would never fully recover from my depression. Perhaps I would never regain my sense of vitality. All I could do was make choices – positive choices – that advanced my story.

I still believed in redemption, but I began to see it as a much smaller-scale endeavour than I once did. I found redemption in simple, everyday experiences that cast a little bit of light into my shadows. Clutching a warm cup of tea. Noticing that my peace lily had produced another flower. Staring into the warm glow of a candle. Watching YouTube videos of husky puppies fighting in the snow. Rebuilding my relationships with old friends. Spending time with my parents. These moments were not grand or extraordinary, but each of them helped to restore my sense of wholeness.

In Japan, there is an ancient art called kintsugi. It is the process of repairing a piece of broken pottery by piecing it back together with gold lacquer. The repair process does not attempt to hide the object's brokenness. Although the gold paste fills the cracks, they are not erased. In fact, they are made even more obvious, highlighted by the gold veins running across the object. Rather than providing a reason to throw it out, the object's brokenness is considered to have made it even more beautiful. Kintsugi teaches us that the cracks don't ruin an object's story, because the cracks *are* the story.

Accept what you can't change.

18. FREEDOM

There's something I haven't told you. Something that happened quite out of the blue, many months before I returned to Wellington. I received an email from Alex Hedley, the New Zealand publisher for HarperCollins. He liked my reporting, and wanted to talk. On the morning of our meeting, I was in a depressive funk. I had been in bed for 18 hours, and woke up next to the crumpled detritus of a McDonald's binge from the night before. I dragged myself out of my flat and trudged down Ponsonby Road to meet Alex at a café. He wanted to know if I had any ideas for a book. I didn't know whether I could go to work that day, let alone whether I could write a book. I told him I would think about it, and then went back home to bed.

Sometimes, during the most boring chapter of a story, there's a plot twist in motion – a twist that you can easily miss if you're not paying attention. In the months after that meeting, I became curious about the idea of putting my memories on paper – examining the story that I had wrapped around my depression, and trying to extract meaning from it. When I decided to take six months off work, I then decided to write *This Is Not How It Ends*. When I started the book, I had no idea how it would end. Given the mental state I was in, I wasn't even sure if I would reach the last chapter, *this* chapter. But I was keen to rewrite my story. As it turned out, my story rewrote me.

*

As a kid, I was shy and sensitive. I struggled to find my place in the world. I didn't know how to process and articulate my emotions, so I bottled them up. When I grew into an adult, I continued living out of the toxic narratives that had formed during my childhood. I believed that my body was defective, that I was unlovable, and that I was no one's priority. I was able to get through life by performing and achieving, but once I moved to Auckland, those strategies began to fail. As my mental health deteriorated, I tried different strategies, hoping to improve my wellbeing. They made very little difference.

My distress had been triggered by major changes in my lifestyle, including taking a new job in a new city, and being separated from my friends and family. When I sought medical help, I was guided down the well-worn path of clinical depression – a path I had never thought I would tread. I believed I had a disorder. I read screeds of information online about the corrosive effect of depression on the human brain. By the time my doctor and psychiatrist encouraged me to take medication, I was convinced that something had gone seriously wrong inside my head. If my mental health didn't improve, I expected that I would take my own life. Was that the depression talking? Actually, I'm pretty sure it was just me.

"Depression" is the word our society has chosen to describe a particular kind of human experience. For four years, I used that word as shorthand for my mental distress. Those ten letters represented all of my unwanted emotions. However, the notion that I had a mental disorder did not serve me well. In fact, it made me helpless. I believed an illness was in control of me, so I thought my decisions didn't (and couldn't) matter. That "illness" became a self-fulfilling prophecy. The more depressed I thought I was, the more depressed I became. The more I was worried about becoming suicidal, the more I was attracted to the idea of ending my own life.

However, when I began to explore my life as a story – through a non-medical lens, it looked very different. I identified two emotions that my character was struggling with. Firstly, I was experiencing loneliness. I was disconnected from the people I loved. Secondly, I was experiencing grief. I was grieving the loss of things that never existed in the first place. The loss of the self-confidence that I never had. The loss of the social connections that I never had. The loss of the relationship and family that I never had. This kind of grief – a longing for the invisible and intangible – is perhaps the most painful kind of grief, because no one else can see what has been taken away from you. Loneliness and grief are not symptoms of a brain disorder; they're normal human emotions. I didn't have to pathologise them.

Over time, I came to the astonishing realisation that my depression was largely the product of a story that I had written for myself. I had constructed a plot about a broken character who would eventually end his life in order to escape his suffering. As the author of that story, I had the power to reclaim it. I could rewrite my past. I could reinvent my character. I could write a more hopeful plot. I could stop trying to control my ending. Through the process of storytelling, I could find meaning in my suffering – even if I couldn't erase it. This offered me a huge amount of freedom. I had written depression into my story, so I also had the power to write it out.

Some people will be outraged by this idea. I can hear them shouting, "Are you telling me that *my* depression isn't real? How do you know that *my* brain isn't broken?" And that's exactly my point. We *don't* know what is happening in our brains. Mental distress takes many forms, and affects each of us in unique ways. I do believe that clinical depression exists, and I know that for some people, a diagnosis and medication will save their lives. If you fit into that group, I'm stoked. But for others, including me, the medical approach to mental distress has been an abject failure. In order to stay alive, we must think beyond diagnostic labels and explore the stories that our lives are built upon.

*

Our language around mental health needs to change. Many of us believe that if someone is not mentally "well", then they must be mentally "unwell" or have a mental "illness". But health is not binary. It's on a spectrum, and it's highly subjective. When it comes to physical health, one woman with a runny nose may describe herself as sick, while another woman would only use that word if she had full-blown influenza. Similarly, just because you're experiencing mental distress, that does not mean you have to identify as being mentally ill or unwell. Experiencing distress doesn't mean you're sick. It just means you're human.

How you describe your mental state is, in itself, a form of storytelling.

You might be wondering, *What about those who have already taken their own lives?* I believe that, for some people, the distress is so overwhelming – and the circumstances of their lives are so complex – that suicide seems like the only option. We all know of people who have died by suicide – friends, family or colleagues. Many of them bravely fought their suicidal thoughts for months or even years. Sadly, we cannot bring those people back. But, if you're reading this book, you're still here. And that means you have the power to make choices. Although you may believe the world will be better off without you, the rest of us actually need you to stick around, because you play an important role in our stories too.

In the same way that we prescribe antidepressants, teach meditation and encourage people to exercise, I believe we can also help people to rewrite their stories. If I sound evangelical – almost fanatical – about this process, well, that's because I am. I reckon we need a story revolution. There's no need to wait for a cancer diagnosis, a redundancy or a marriage breakup before working on your story. Your self-development goals do not have to be determined by the crises that confront you. We can be proactive and take control of our stories at any time. The power of storytelling could change your life – and perhaps even save it. There's a good chance it saved mine.

*

The Marlborough Sounds, at the top of the South Island, is a piece of Kiwi paradise. When Captain Cook arrived there in 1770, he was aboard the HMS *Endeavour*. When I arrived in March 2020, a humble water taxi was my vessel. Tommy and I travelled to the Sounds for a hike, to mark ten years of our friendship. But really, the trip was a celebration of survival – for both of us. We had made it through one of the worst years of our lives. I was three months into my break from work. Tommy had just quit his job as a newspaper reporter, and was heading back to university to study counselling. His own mental health journey had motivated him to help other people to work through their challenges.

As we walked the Queen Charlotte Track, there was no one in sight – other than a weka that popped its head out of the bush and followed us along the path. We talked about all the things we were grateful for. Grateful for our friendship. Grateful for healthy bodies and strong minds. Grateful for the resources that allowed us to make choices. But as we relaxed in nature, we knew the world was beginning to spin out of control. Covid-19 had just arrived in New Zealand. This would be our last holiday together for a very long time. On our way back to Wellington, Prime Minister Jacinda Ardern announced the creation of four alert levels. New Zealand was at alert level two. Just days later, the whole country went to level four – and into lockdown.

I hunkered down, alone, in my little apartment. In my former life, the idea of being trapped in a room for four weeks would have pushed me over the edge. But when the lockdown began, I wasn't worried. While "social distancing" and "self-isolation" were new concepts for most people, I felt like I had already been practising them for months. My lifestyle became the new normal for five million New Zealanders, and suddenly it didn't seem so weird after all. Of course, I was still visited by loneliness and grief. They came in waves – some days lapping at my feet, other days threatening to overwhelm me. But I had learnt to stand my ground.

During the lockdown, I found out that I was a finalist for Broadcast Journalist of the Year at the Voyager Media Awards. It was ironic, because while the coronavirus story was unfolding, I was missing in action. While my colleagues were covering the biggest news event in a generation, I was sitting in my apartment doing jigsaw puzzles, eating marshmallow eggs and writing this book.

And there was nowhere else I wanted to be. I watched my colleagues on TV, reporting on the pandemic with professionalism and dedication. I was surprised to discover that I wasn't jealous at all. I didn't miss my job – in fact, I felt relieved that I didn't have to do it.

And so it was that I came to an unexpected decision: to resign. When I took my six-month break, I had planned to return to Auckland. But with enough distance and space, I began to wonder: Who would I be *without* television? And who might I become? I know that I will always be a storyteller, and journalism still brings me a lot of joy. I will continue to work in the media. But I also want to teach other people how to tell their own stories, through workshops and coaching. I am heading into a new chapter – a daunting and unfamiliar one. But I am willing to trust the process.

When I announced my resignation on Twitter, I had a phone call from a reporter, asking about the story behind my departure. Had I been pushed out? Did TVNZ cut my job? Was I leaving because of the coronavirus? I assured her: No, it was my decision – the right one for me. Half an hour later, my face was on the news website's home page along with the headline "SUNDAY REPORTER QUITS TVNZ". I received hundreds of beautiful messages, mostly from strangers who wanted to wish me well and tell me how my stories had affected and inspired them. As usual, the online trolls popped their heads up too. *So what?* wrote Edward. *Good riddance,* wrote Jonathan. *One more biased know-it-all gone,* wrote Gail. For a moment, a dark cloud passed over me. But it didn't stick around.

*

This book is full of true stories from my own life, and from the lives of others. Everything in the previous chapters really happened – but, as the author, I have chosen how to interpret those events. There are things I have emphasised, and things I have left out. There are things I have expanded on, and things I have condensed. The story you have just read is the story that I now choose to live. I choose this story over the story of depression. I choose this story over my feelings of frustration, despair and hopelessness. Some days, I have to make these choices over and over again – hour by hour, or minute by minute, if necessary. But I know that my story is strong enough to carry me through.

I no longer believe that a good story needs a happy ending. Rather, a good story is one that transforms its main character for the better. Despite all the pain I've experienced over the past four years, I know that none of it has been wasted. Having survived mental distress,

I am stronger, wiser and more compassionate. The twists and turns in my life have led me to places that I would never have chosen to go. Despite the darkness that has dominated my story in recent times, I still believe in the possibility of redemption. And no matter what happens next, I know that suffering cannot kill me.

I always wondered what it would be like to reach these final pages. I desperately wanted to be able to tie all the loose threads together in a bright red bow, and shout, "Look! This is how it all turned out!" But to do so would be to lie. The reality is that my life is still a collection of loose threads. I still live with a lot of uncertainty about what my future will look like, who I will spend it with, and what my contribution to the world will be. But I'm learning to be okay with that. I'm learning that it's okay to have pages that are still blank, and words that are yet to be written. As far as I know, time is on my side.

My story will have a final chapter – but this isn't it. I don't know which forces will bring my story to its conclusion, or when that will happen. By the time the ink is dry on the last sentence, I'll be somewhere else, far away – and the pain will be over. But when the end does come, I know that I will not have authored it. Between this page and the very last, I will spend my days keeping my story alive. I will write good dialogue, create beautiful scenes, and hopefully make cool cameos in other people's stories too. There is so much light in the world, and I am starting to notice it again. But I am also not afraid of darkness anymore. The dark is where the monsters live – but it's also where the best stories come from.

Stories have the power to heal.

EPILOGUE

Six months. That's how long it has been since I finished writing this book. Looking back on it now, I feel like I'm reading someone else's story. I almost don't recognise the person who wrote most of this book. That's because my life has changed so much. It has changed for the better.

Rewriting my story had a profound impact on me. It helped me to realise that my brain wasn't broken, that I didn't have an "illness", and that I wasn't going crazy. I was just experiencing an intense period of mental distress – a period of suffering. By changing my story, I was able to make important changes in my life. The biggest risk I have ever taken – leaving Auckland and leaving my TV job – has paid off. I'm still telling stories on TV, in print and online. But now, I'm in control of my time and my workload.

In my own story, I have worked hard to become the best character I can be. Every day, I make decisions based on my values. When I face conflict, I choose to embrace it, rather than run away from it. I have accepted that suffering is part of life, and that my pain can transform me for the better. Rewriting my story has allowed me to heal – mentally, emotionally and spiritually. For the first time in four years, I am functioning at 100 per cent. I still have really bad days, but they're uncommon. In all areas of my life, I feel stronger than ever. A few months ago, I could never have imagined writing those words.

I spend a lot of time speaking to businesses and community groups about the power of storytelling, and how our stories influence our mental wellbeing. I'm teaching people how to apply the principles of good storytelling in their own lives. Some people have told me that I have challenged them to think differently about mental distress. Others have told me that my story has contributed to their own healing. That's humbling. It reminds me that my story has value, and I can use it to help others.

Just because I have overcome my distress, that doesn't mean it was okay. I can't find a silver lining in the trauma, pain and upheaval that came from that period. Distress is awful, and suicidality is horrendous. But here's the thing: all of our experiences can enrich our stories. In the world of storytelling, nothing is wasted – not even the worst stuff. I know that my story is more powerful because of everything that I have fought, endured and survived.

When I was in the depths of despair, I was irritated by people who would say, "Trust me – it gets better." When you're struggling, those words sound hollow. And I know that. But you know what? You just need to trust me, because life does get better. And, in my experience, a little bit of trust goes a very long way.

Jehan Casinader
September 2020

THANKS

When I was a young reporter, I submitted an article to a current affairs magazine. The editor sent it back to me, covered with notes in red. He had pulled my story apart and exposed how poorly it was constructed. "I find writing very hard," the editor said. "You should too. The result will be better writing." His feedback was brutal, but it taught me that telling a good story is *meant* to be challenging. Writing this book was the hardest storytelling experience of my life.

I couldn't have done it without support. I'm grateful to Sam Newton for being patient and kind, and helping me to explore my mental distress in a fresh way; to Andrew Dalton for giving me a reason to laugh, even on the really tough days; and to Kevin Denholm for his wisdom and encouragement. I would also like to thank others who have supported me: Stephen Heron, Jerram Watts, Dave Grant, Dan Mazengarb, Samuel Wood and

Brooke Livingston. To the team at TVNZ – the talented producers, cameramen and editors I have worked with – thank you for helping me to tell great stories, and for giving me the confidence to be myself. Thanks to my parents, Ravi and Saro, and my brother, Prashan, for their constant love and support.

Thanks to Alex Hedley and the awesome team at HarperCollins for giving me the opportunity to write this book, and to Kimberley Davis for handling the manuscript with such care. Finally, thank you for reading it. I hope *This Is Not How It Ends* has allowed you to see your life a little differently. I would love to hear about what you took away from this book. Let me know: **hello@jehancasinader.co.nz**. Take care, and remember: It ain't over till it's over.

STORY GUIDE

This guide briefly summarises the key messages in *This Is Not How It Ends*. It also includes questions that will help you to explore your own story.

Make a cup of tea and grab your journal or a blank sheet of paper. It's really useful to write things down, and you can come back to your notes later on.

Consider sharing this process with a trusted friend or family member, or your counsellor or therapist. They will be able to ask you extra questions, and may offer a fresh perspective.

I. RECLAIM YOUR STORY
THINK:
- You're the main character in your life story. You're also the author of that story.
- Although you cannot control most of the events that happen in your life, you can control your

interpretation – the story – that is wrapped around those events.
- Our stories become our reality. They profoundly influence how we see the world, and how we see ourselves.
- Having a coherent, meaningful story about your life can contribute to your psychological wellbeing, even when life gets tough.
- Your story is not fixed. It is not objectively true or false, right or wrong. It can always be changed.
- No one else can write your story. Authorship is solely your responsibility.

ASK:
- What is the story that I am currently living out of?
- What's happening in that story? Where does the plot seem to be heading?
- Does my story feature more "redemption" or "contamination"?
- How does my story affect the way I view myself?
- Is it possible to write a different kind of story for my life? What impact could that have on my mental health?

II. REWRITE YOUR PAST

THINK:
- The source of your pain lies in your past. Toxic narratives begin in childhood, often because of traumatic events.
- The narratives that take hold of us as children continue to affect us as adults.
- Silence is harmful. If a story is suppressed, it often finds a way of expressing itself through dysfunction or distress.
- Many of us feel pressure to conform to dominant cultural scripts. Those scripts work for some people, but not for everyone.
- All of us have experienced pain, and we shouldn't be ashamed of it. Our scars do not ruin our stories; our scars are part of our stories.

ASK:
- When did pain first show up in my life? How did I respond to it?
- What have been the most significant traumatic experiences in my life?
- Which narratives came from these experiences? How do these narratives affect me today?
- Can I write a different story around the painful events in my past?

- Which cultural scripts have I tried to follow? Have they helped me, or harmed me?
- What would my life look like if I stopped trying to follow these scripts?
- How can I become more comfortable showing my scars to other people? What are the benefits of doing that – for me, and for them?

III. REINVENT YOUR CHARACTER
THINK:
- You can choose what kind of character to play in your story.
- A character's identity is much more than their feelings. Your feelings – no matter how powerful they are – do not define you.
- Characters have the capacity to endure huge amounts of suffering. When faced with adversity, they usually discover that they are much stronger than they thought.
- Every good character must want something. Sometimes, other people's needs provide an even greater source of motivation than our own needs.
- Loneliness is a killer. Every character needs to be connected to other characters.

ASK:
- What kind of character am I playing in my story?
- Do my feelings have too much power over me?
- How can I refocus on the core parts of my identity – including my skills, interests, personality and sense of humour?
- How has my suffering changed me as a character? What has it taught me about myself?
- Where does my motivation come from? Is it strong enough, or do I need to find another source of motivation?
- Who are the supporting characters in my story, and what roles do they play? What roles do I play in their stories?
- When I look at my life right now, what would a good character do? How would a good character respond to the challenges that I currently face?

IV. RESHAPE YOUR PLOT

THINK:
- Conflict is a vital part of any story. It develops the characters and moves the story forward. Your story will never be free of conflict.
- The purpose of a good story is not to have a happy ending. Rather, the purpose is that the main character is transformed in a positive way.

- You can always find meaning in your story by returning to your beliefs and values. Exploring spirituality helps you to identify what your beliefs and values are.
- Stories are contagious. We are heavily influenced – both positively and negatively – by the stories around us.
- Our stories affect the emotional lives of our friends, family and colleagues.

ASK:
- Is there conflict in my story? What form does it take?
- How have I responded to that conflict? How has it transformed me as a character?
- What are my beliefs and values, and how do they shape the meaning of my story?
- Is there another way to interpret what is currently happening in my story? Are there other perspectives available to me?
- How have I been influenced by other people's stories, and by the stories in popular culture? Are those stories helping me, or harming me?
- How is my story affecting the stories of people around me?

V. RELEASE YOUR ENDING

THINK:

- Rather than trying to control the ending of your story, you can instead focus on being a good character and writing a creative plot.
- Even when life is hard, you can trust the process of storytelling to help you make sense of what is happening in your life.
- Rather than trying to erase suffering, you can learn to accept it.
- Things don't have to be fixed, cured or tidied away for a story to be meaningful.
- Our stories can carry us through tough times. Our stories can help us to heal.

ASK:

- Am I trying to control my ending? Can I release control of it? What impact would that have on my mental health?
- Rather than focusing on how my story will end, how can I be a better character? How can I write a better plot?
- Can I accept the things I cannot change?
- When my story does come to an end, what kind of character do I want to be? And what kind of story do I hope to have lived?

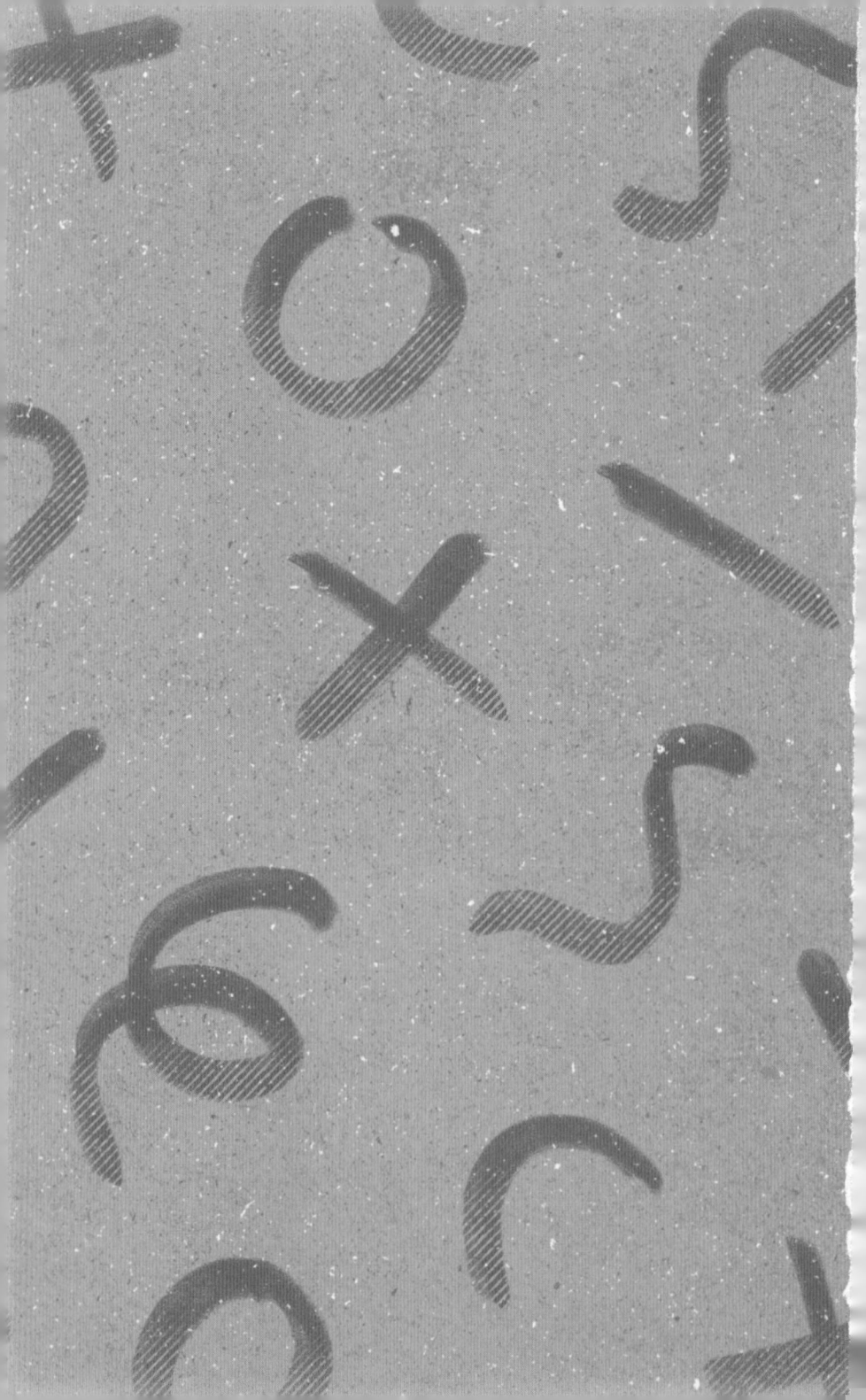